JEMIMA *for Pauline Blackburn*

13 × 22.5 cm. Watercolour. September
1856. William and Margaret in Hugh's
study at Roshven.

JEMIMA

THE PAINTINGS AND MEMOIRS OF A VICTORIAN LADY
EDITED AND WITH AN INTRODUCTION
BY ROBERT FAIRLEY

CANONGATE

First published in Great Britain in 1988 by Canongate
Publishing Limited, 17 Jeffrey Street, Edinburgh. Intro-
duction © 1988 Robert Fairley. Memoirs © 1988 Alan
Blackburn and Robert Fairley.

The publishers gratefully acknowledge permission to
reprint passages from *Grey Ghosts and Voices* by May
Wedderburn Cannan, Roundwood Press (1976). They
also acknowledge subsidy towards the publication of this
volume from The Scottish Arts Council.

British Library Cataloguing in Publication Data
Blackburn, Jemima, 1823–1909
    Jemima : paintings and memoirs of a
    Victorian lady
    1. Great Britain. Blackburn, Jemima, 1823–
    1909
    I. Title II. Fairley, Robert
    941.081′092′4
    ISBN 0-86241-186-6

Colour separation by Marshall Thompson, Edinburgh.
Typeset by BAS Printers, Over Wallop, Hampshire
Printed and bound by Butler & Tanner Frome, Somerset.

Opposite
11.25 × 13 cm. Watercolour. 18 July 1857.
A family group painted during one of
Andrew Wedderburn's rare visits to
Roshven; on this occasion he stayed only
a few days as he felt himself too isolated
from news of the Indian Mutiny.

Frontispiece
31 × 22.5 cm. Watercolour and pencil.
'Long eared owl.' *Birds from Moidart*,
p. 29 (detail only).

ACKNOWLEDGEMENTS

Without the support and encouragement and friendship of the entire Blackburn family this volume would never have seen the light of day. Mrs Pauline Blackburn provided the initial spur and her interest, enthusiasm and practical assistance (not least the regular provision of lunch!) have been a constant source of inspiration. Mr and Mrs Alan Blackburn, Mr and Mrs Nigel Blackburn, Mr Ninian Blackburn, Mr Jamie Blackburn, Miss Felicity Blackburn, Miss Catriona Blackburn, Miss Vicky Blackburn, Mr Hugh Blackburn, Mr and Mrs Robert Maclean, Mrs Elizabeth Grey and Mrs Veronica Parker all provided much valuable information.

I am grateful for permission to reproduce paintings from the collections of Mr Alan Blackburn, Sir John Barren, the Hon. Mrs Monro, Mr and Mrs D. Farr and Brigadier Wedderburn Maxwell.

I have been greatly helped by all the people who have allowed me to view their Blackburn paintings and those who have written to me with relevent information. In this respect I mention Miss Jean Burns, Mr Patrick Bourne, Miss Karen Brennan, Mr David Black, Mrs Cameron Head, Sir John Clerk, Mr John Dye, Mr and Mrs R. I. Fairley, Dr R. I. Fairley, Miss Anne Fairley, Prof. R. V. Jones, Mr and Mrs L. Lambourne, the late Mr (Tom) MacDonald, the late Miss Catriona Maclean of Ardgour, Mr A. P. Maclean, Mr D. Macrae, Mr H. Marwick, Lady Delia Millar, Mrs Alison Peaker, Dr J. S. Reid, Mr H. Radcliffe, Mr L. Schaaf, Mrs N. Stewart, Mr I. Thornber, Dr I. Tolstoy, Mr P. White and Mr A. Wilson.

The staff of the British Museum Print Room, the British Library, the British Museum of Natural History, Glasgow University, Cambridge University, Aberdeen University's Dept of Natural Philosophy, the Indian Record Office, the National Photographic Archive, the National Library of Scotland, the National Portrait Gallery, the National Maritime Museum, the Royal Library (Windsor) and the West Highland Museum have all been most helpful.

I have been fortunate in having two excellent typists, Mrs Anne Dye who tackled the formidable task of typing the decyphered 'memoirs' and Miss Jean Duckman who decyphered my introduction. My thanks also must go to Mr Malcolm Gillespie of the Sea Fish Industry Authority and Mr Gordon Rae and Mr Steve Bracken of Marine Harvest for the loan of their photocopying facilities.

I gratefully acknowledge the assistance of the Scottish Arts Council, and place on record my warmest thanks to *all* at Canongate.

These acknowledgements would not be complete without recording my gratitude to Fiona Marwick who, having helped decypher the memoirs, has lived with every aspect of this book for the last four years, without her help much of it could not have been accomplished.

Rob Fairley, *Lochailort* 1988

INTRODUCTION

IT WAS ONE OF THE strangest requests that the Duke of
Wellington had ever received. He had been strolling in the gardens
close to Apsley House a few days after his seventy first birthday
when he was approached by five teenage girls. One, smaller but more
elegantly dressed than the others, fixed him with strangely brilliant
eyes and asked in a decidedly Scots voice if he would be so kind as
to give names to two frogs she had found while on a visit to the
country. The Duke thought for a moment before, perhaps inevitably,
suggesting, 'Call them Monsieur and Madame'.

This Scots girl, Jemima Wedderburn, was to become one of the
Victorian age's foremost illustrators, achieving widespread recognition under the initials J.B. or her married name, Mrs Hugh Blackburn. She was a watercolourist of outstanding technical ability whose
keen sense of observation gives us a faithful and evocative picture
of her life in nineteenth century Scotland. Her lyrical depictions of
country life in the West Highlands, her meticulous ornithological
illustrations, and the enchanting vignettes of her own day to day
experiences, sprang from a profound intellectual curiosity which
found expression through a lively and vivid imagination. She was anything but a Victorian country house lady who looked upon watercolour
painting as a pleasant way to pass the time. She painted and drew,
almost obsessively, all her life. Rare was the day she did not put brush
or pencil to paper.

Her family and friends preserved her work in bound albums, some
forty of which survive, having been passed down through various lines
of descent. All have been treasured and cared for, though few owners
realised that what they possessed was only a part of a larger corpus.
These albums (containing for the most part work never intended for
publication) when viewed as a whole are an extraordinarily vivid and
personal visual diary for the years from 1837 until 1901, precisely
the period of Victoria's reign.

Jemima was born in Edinburgh, the youngest daughter of James
and Isabella Wedderburn. Her mother, known in her youth as the
'Daisy of Pentland' by Edinburgh society, was a member of the noted

Facing page
21 × 15.8 cm. Jemima Blackburn,
photographed c. 1852, possibly by
Alinari of Florence.

13.5 × 12.5 cm. Ink and Watercolour. 3 May 1840. The Duke of Wellington naming the frogs.

Clerk of Penicuik family, and attracted great attention for her beauty. Her daughter inherited her mother's small stature, clear features and, according to one writer, 'beautiful forehead'. James Wedderburn was descended from one of Scotland's oldest and most distinguished families. He had been educated at Musselburgh Grammar School, which at the time was well known, and rose rapidly through the ranks of the legal profession to become, at an unusually early age, Solicitor-General for Scotland, a post he held, it must be admitted, with no great distinction. In about 1820 he purchased 31 Heriot Row, a large house in the centre of a recently completed street on the fringe of Edinburgh's New Town. The house, becoming known to the family as 'auld 31', needed to be large, for seven years of marriage had produced six children, James, Janet, George, Jean, John and Andrew. They lived happily and in some comfort until November 1822 when Mr Wedderburn, on a visit to his sister, the Countess of Selkirk, at St. Mary's Isle near Kirkcudbright, was caught in a violent storm and contracted a chill, from which after a few days' illness he died. Six months later, on 1 May 1823, Jemima was born.

Her early childhood was overshadowed by the loss of her father and beset by intermittent illness. She was a delicate child, and until the age of nine spent much time indoors or in bed. During one period of convalescence the family doctor (the noted James Abercrombie) was consulted on the matter of his young patient's education. He prescribed drawing as a suitable therapy and forbade book lessons. A dormant talent was aroused, and before long Jemima was drawing on any piece of paper that could be found. Her mother, no doubt glad to have a means of keeping her young invalid occupied, encouraged her by buying sketch books which she rapidly filled with drawings of animals and birds. Those that survive also contain drawings by elder brothers, sisters, aunts and uncles. Jemima, like many children, was obviously adept at persuading any visiting adult to 'Draw for me'.

The Wedderburn family lived quietly and conservatively, travelling rarely, and then only to Penicuik or Craigflower in Fife, the home of Mr Wedderburn's brother Andrew. Mrs Wedderburn, despite long periods of illness, brought up her children well. The boys were educated at Edinburgh Academy, and in an era when education for young girls was often restricted, she was unusually progressive in her outlook. Her daughters were taught to read when very young, and by the age of ten Jemima was reading Paley's *Natural Theology*. Her eldest brother James was studying surgery, and encouraged by him she began dissecting mice to examine and study the movements of their muscles, knowledge which she quickly applied to her drawing.

William IV died in 1837 and was succeeded by his niece Victoria. The coronation the following year marked the end of the Wedderburns' quiet and orderly family life. James, who on qualifying in 1835 had joined the Coldstream Guards as an assistant surgeon, was posted to Canada. John entered the military service of the East India Company; and on 10 April Janet married a young Edinburgh lawyer, James McKenzie, and Jean married Peter Blackburn, the eldest son of John Blackburn of Killearn. The joint wedding was followed, more unusually, by a joint honeymoon on which, even more unusually, Jemima accompanied her sisters.

John Blackburn had made a fortune as a young man in the Jamaican sugar trade. He returned to Glasgow in 1810 leaving behind a number of 'particoloured descendants' whom the family had to support for many years until, toward the end of the century, the line eventually died out. A growing abhorrence of the slave trade caused him to free all the slaves who worked on his plantation when he departed. Those who wished it he settled in Nova Scotia, some as was the custom adopting his surname. In 1811, at the age of fifty five, he married Rebecca Leslie Gillies, then aged twenty three. She was the daughter of a Church of Scotland minister and a grandniece of the renowned mathematician Colin MacLaurin, and by all accounts an exceptionally attractive woman. They raised a family of six boys, Peter, Colin, John, Andrew, Robert and Hugh, and two girls, Isabella and Helen, the youngest, who was born in September 1826 when her father was approaching his seventy first birthday.

In 1814 he purchased the old estate of Killearn, some sixteen miles north west of Glasgow, and built a new house which was thenceforth known as Killearn House, while the original he allowed to fall into decay. As time progressed his family's education became a matter of some importance, and he resolved that in the case of his sons it should be started at Edinburgh Academy. Accordingly he bought two sites in Queen Street, at that time a fashionable residential part of Edinburgh's New Town, and built a single house. The family then moved to Edinburgh during term time and back to Killearn for the rest of the year.

The Wedderburn and Blackburn families, though distantly related, seem to have had little or no communication until the boys started at the Academy. James and George Wedderburn and Peter, Andrew and Colin Blackburn were all at school together, James and Andrew in the same class for three years. The younger boys, John and Andrew Wedderburn and Hugh Blackburn, were also contemporaries, and it

Detail
26.2 × 15 cm. Watercolour.
Constructing a large balloon on the
staircase in the old house at Killearn.
Left to right: Andrew Blackburn,
Jemima, Peter Blackburn, Hugh.

seems likely that it was here that the real friendship between the families developed. The New Town of Edinburgh is not large, and the Blackburn boys would have had to pass the end of Heriot Row on their way to school.

After the marriage of Jean and Peter, Jemima began to spend a considerable amount of time at Killearn. She became very friendly with Helen Blackburn and happily joined in all the family activities. Both Killearn and Penicuik gave her freedom to indulge her passion for riding, a pursuit which gave her pleasure well into old age. Towards the end of her life she wrote that 'of all things I liked riding best'. She was an extremely accomplished horsewoman, and as a child taught her ponies to perform remarkable tricks.

Hugh Blackburn was born on 2 July 1823 and was, therefore, only

Detail
22.5 × 14.3 cm. Watercolour. Inflating the large balloon in the hall at Killearn. John Clerk-Maxwell on the balcony and on the floor. Left to right: Andrew Blackburn, James Clerk-Maxwell, Peter and Hugh Blackburn with an unidentified figure behind the balloon.

a couple of months younger than Jemima. He was a quiet and studious lad with wide-ranging interests. He possessed a four-volume set of Hutton's *Mathematical Recreations*, books which were far from being as dull as they sounded for they detailed hundreds of simple games, plans and experiments which enabled the practically-minded to construct a large number of fascinating machines, toys and scientific devices. Jemima's drawings catalogue several of his 'inventions', most notably a series of hot air balloons, in which each successful flight seems to have prompted the manufacture of an even larger model.

8 × 11.5 cm. Ink and watercolour over pencil. An attempt to take his horse to be photographed (1838). The earliest indication that photography figured among the many scientific experiments carried out by Hugh and his brothers at Killearn.

Finally one was made so large that it had to be hung from the upper stair banister in Killearn to enable the finishing touches to be put to it. It flew perhaps too well, for the drawings show it vanishing over a distant horizon while the whole family pursue it through hedges and ditches and over dykes and fences. His elder brothers had friends among the scientific community, and he was always keen to try out the latest modification to the basic experiments given in his Hutton. The study of optics had fascinated him for some years, and by the mid to late 1830's he had begun to try and make photographs.

William Henry Fox Talbot had formulated a process of making photographs in 1834–5 but found other things to occupy his mind, and did nothing about his discovery until in 1839 news came from France of a process which seemed identical to his own. Talbot, not realising that the method devised by Daguerre was in fact very different, hastened to publish details of his work, the paper appearing in February 1839. The previous year Jemima had painted a small watercolour showing John Blackburn taking his horse to be photographed. Though the evidence is scant, fragmentary, and much of it circumstantial, it seems that Hugh had formulated his own method of making photographs, but they did not prove fully permanent. Hutton gave him sufficient information to build a simple camera obscura and therefore to form a simple camera, but until the publication of Fox Talbot's paper he had little access to information on the chemistry of the subject and had to rely on hearsay and experimentation. His comparative lack of interest in chemistry, and his desire always to try out new ideas, led to many such failures over the years.

Jemima was fascinated by these experiments, and indeed it seems that Hugh made efforts to reproduce some of her drawings by photographic methods. Prompted by this she began to try other means of reproduction, and taught herself the art of making woodcuts and wood engravings. Her first efforts in this medium, being inevitably of dogs and horses, show remarkable virtuosity and helped to persuade her to think of her drawing as something more than just an amusing pastime.

The Wedderburn family had a pleasant custom of gathering all its members together and having a party on the evening before any of them were to leave on a long journey. The meal they ate on such occasions always included oysters so, in the parlance of the family, the event became known as an 'oyster festival'. On 13 March 1840 they met in 'auld 31' for such a festival and to wish Jemima *bon voyage*. Mrs Wedderburn had decided that to 'finish' her education she should spend some time in London, and had arranged for her to spend three months with her aunt and uncle, the Wedderburn Colviles, at their house in Curzon Street. Before she left, her mother made her promise to send home a drawing every day, such a scheme only recently having become feasible by the introduction of the penny post two months earlier. Jemima kept her promise, missing only two days and amply making up for this by producing more than one on several occasions.

Andrew and Mary Colville had four sons and twelve daughters. They made their cousin from Scotland very welcome, rapidly and excitedly planning a full schedule for the coming weeks. Uppermost in this was to be an introduction to the Duke of Wellington, with whom the Colvile girls had become friendly. There is a curious disparity between the two accounts Jemima gave of this meeting. One in her memoir reports it as a fairly ordinary and straightforward affair. The other she related to John Macleod, a close friend in later life, who wrote in a short volume of *Reminiscences* that she 'wished to be introduced to the Duke of Wellington and apparently was unwilling to be beholden to her aristocratic friends for the coveted honour. She made use of a stratagem to gain her end that was characteristically original. It was entirely successful, although, like some more important strategy, it might have miscarried. She made a caricature of His Grace, which she sent him, and he thought it so clever that he actually visited her and ever afterwards sent her an invitation to his Waterloo Ball.' The Duke showed great interest in Jemima's painting, inviting her and the Colvile girls to see his paintings in Apsley House, and on another occasion taking Jemima to see his horse so that they could compare a portrait she had drawn of it with the animal itself.

The Colviles were acquainted with many of the most prominent figures in London society. James, the eldest of her cousins and a successful young lawyer, took Jemima under his wing, and introduced her to poets, artists and connoisseurs, as well as to the sights of London. In the evenings they went to the theatre or the opera. She cared little for music, 'quite' enjoying Italian opera only 'when the acting was good'. Much more to her taste was a visit to Astley's circus. Ever since the days when she had trained the ponies at Killearn and Penicuik she had clung to a girlish fancy to become a circus girl. Had this wish 'been more than temporary', wrote a contemporary, 'and circumstances made her pursue the vocation, she would have been the most brilliant circus girl of the century'.

When she had been in London for about five weeks she was

Overleaf
22.8 × 27.5 cm. Watercolour. 'Sparrow Hawk.' Illustration from *The Instructive Picture Book*, 7th edition, pl. XIV and *Birds from Moidart*, p. 25.

16 ᵗʰ Feby

23 × 15.2 cm. Watercolour. Portrait of
Andrew Wedderburn painted during
his first leave.

delighted to receive a weekend visit from her brother Andrew, who
was at Haileybury College in Herfordshire studying to enter the
Madras Civil Service. They had always been very close, shared the
same interests in painting and natural history, and had the same sense
of humour. Andrew had found the work at Haileybury much harder
than he had expected, and suffered terribly from homesickness. In
a letter written to Jemima before she left for London he describes
his predicament: 'I have been about a fortnight at the College and
you may imagine that it is not very pleasant at first .... We have
a great deal to do, not so much in having lectures every day as in

Detail
13.3 × 13.3 cm. Watercolour. Helen
Blackburn and Jemima fishing.

preparing for an examination at the end of term. We have horrid long
compositions in English to write every week . . . . I found great difficulty in beginning the Sanskrit grammar which is a nice little book
of about a stone in weight. We go posting through it at a great rate,
so that after six or seven lectures we are expected to read a book before
many know the letters . . . . I hope you will write me a nice long letter
weekly as it is a great comfort to hear from home.' The weekend must
have passed all too quickly for them both.

April 29 was the Duke of Wellington's birthday, and the cousins
met him in the gardens close to Apsley House to wish him the compli-
ments of the day before returning to Curzon Street to prepare for
an expedition into the country the following day. This was the trip
on which the frogs Monsieur and Madame were to be captured. The
days and weeks slipped by, and before long it was time for Jemima
to take her leave and return north.

On her return to Edinburgh she found it hard to settle into the
old dull routines that Scottish, or at least Edinburgh, society deman-
ded. She missed the company of her cousins and had only her elder
brother George to accompany her on rides, or to the theatre. He had
been admitted Writer to the Signet at the end of January 1840. 'A
young man about town and a humorist of a different order,' he was
not the ideal escort for his sister. Eventually Mrs Wedderburn became
so exasperated at having a moody and unsettled teenager around the
house that she packed her off to Killearn.

Everything about Killearn suited Jemima. She and Helen went
fishing and for long walks, helped in the garden, and rode for miles
in the surrounding countryside. In the evenings she was surrounded
by intellectual conversation that covered a wide variety of topics but
usually settled on the Blackburns' love of legends, fairy and folk tales,
ballads and old songs. These evenings spent listening to the story,
or song, telling of an ancient hero or magical event prompted her
to try and illustrate some of them. It is interesting to note that during
this period any time spent in the company of Hugh Blackburn led
to her experimenting further with print-making techniques, and

several of these early 'fable' illustrations constitute her first attempts at engraving.

In the autumn of 1840 Astley's circus visited Edinburgh. Jemima was greatly impressed by the American lion tamer, Van Amburgh, and painted several watercolour portraits of him, and also produced at least one engraving taken from one of the paintings.

The following year Andrew completed his studies at Haileybury, his problems with Sanskrit seemingly short-lived for he left with the Sanskrit medal. He was not due to report in Madras until April 1842 and therefore had several months to fill. It was suggested that he, George, Jemima, and their mother should use the time to go on a tour of northern Europe together. They stayed with the family of her uncle, Sir George Clerk, M.P. in London for a couple of days and naturally visited the zoo. Mrs Wedderburn was persuaded to have a ride on an elephant, and the rest of the family in high good humour joined her. This set the tone for the tour, and for the next fortnight they visited Antwerp, then travelled through Belgium (getting lost in Brussels) on to Germany, and as far as the Prussian border before returning to Heidelberg, where George and Andrew settled the accounts and took leave of their mother and sister, intending to travel on to the South of France, from where Andrew began his journey to India.

Mrs Wedderburn had planned to visit her brother John Clerk-Maxwell on the way home. He lived at Glenlair, near Corsock, in a remote corner of Galloway in south west Scotland. They decided to travel by train, the first time either of them had been on one, to Leicester, from where they caught the mail coach to Dumfries. Here they had to hire another coach to take them to Corsock, the entire journey being accomplished in a little under twenty four hours.

John Clerk had inherited the Galloway estate of Middlebie (which had come into the family through marriage) and added Maxwell to his name. He was by profession a lawyer, though his practice was by all accounts desultory. He was a quiet, intelligent, but somewhat ineffectual man who, having lived with his mother until her death, married late, he being thirty nine and Frances Cay thirty four. She was an entertaining and intelligent woman who spurred him into doing something with the Middlebie estate, and eventually he designed and built the manor of Glenlair. Their first child did not survive, but the second, a son, James, had been born on 13 June 1831. Frances Clerk-Maxwell became seriously ill soon after, probably with cancer, and in a desperate effort to save her life an operation was performed, this before the advent of anaesthetics. She suffered terrible agony and died in December 1839.

In Victorian times the educating of very young children was largely the province of women; however John Clerk-Maxwell himself undertook the education of his small son. James had an outstanding memory and tremendous energy, and as he followed his father around the estate was always enquiring 'What's the go o' that?'; 'What does it do?' Realising his own limitations Mr Clerk-Maxwell eventually engaged a tutor, a man who believed that to make young boys absorb learning

Opposite. Detail
13.8 × 21.5 cm. Watercolour. 22 September 1841. The Wedderburn family at the Russian border during their tour of Europe.

Opposite
10 × 14 cm. Watercolour. 13 October 1841. John Clerk-Maxwell welcoming Jemima and Mrs Blackburn to Glenlair.

they had to be physically coerced. Surprisingly, it took James's father two years to realise what was going on, and then with considerable soul-searching he decided to send James to the Academy in Edinburgh, where he could lodge with his aunt in Heriot Row.

Edinburgh was an unhealthy place, especially in winter when the smell of coal smoke hung everywhere. Its nickname of 'Auld Reekie' had not been gained for nothing. James, coming from the heather- and bracken-covered hills of Galloway, suffered more than his fair share of colds and coughs during his first winter in the city. During the long winter evenings he and Jemima amused themselves by making several mechanical toys. One, a phenakistoscope, was much in vogue, though very expensive in its commercial form. It took the form of a disc with figures drawn in carefully graduated positions. This, when turned in front of a viewing aperture, gave the figures the illusion of continuous movement. James contrived to make the mechanical parts, and Jemima painted the discs. The best of these show a lively imagination and illustrate, typically, a circus performer leaping from a horse's back through a hoop. Jemima mentions in her memoir that they made other toys together, but it is difficult to determine exactly what form they took.

At the age of fourteen James formulated an ingenious arrangement of pins and strings which he used for constructing ellipses. The paper which he wrote on this discovery was shown by his father to Professor James Forbes of Edinburgh University, a physicist, glaciologist, and mountaineer of some distinction. Forbes, deciding that Maxwell's results were indeed original, presented them at a meeting of the Royal Society of Edinburgh, adding the comment that Clerk-Maxwell's methods were simpler than the scheme used by Descartes, and that these were the same ovals as discussed by Newton and Huygens. (A footnote in J. G. Crowther's essay on Clerk-Maxwell rightly exclaims, 'What names to appear in the discussion of a schoolboy's discovery'.) He was one of those rare people who through talent, perseverance, and that elusive and mysterious quality we call genius, completely revolutionised his field of work so as to alter for all time our view of the world. He was to become one of science's great original thinkers, ranking alongside Newton and Einstein. His theory of electromagnetism holds the seeds of all contemporary physics, and no discovery of the Victorian age, with the possible exception of Darwin's theory of evolution, is of such intrinsic importance.

Young James Clerk-Maxwell appreciated the stimulating atmosphere at Killearn and his talent with words and skill in composing serio-comic verses saw him readily welcomed to the fireside. In Hugh Blackburn he found a young man who could appreciate and enjoy his enthusiasms and who was prepared to help with experiments, no matter how wildly improbable or impractical the original idea might seem. Hugh had the intellectual curiosity to follow closely advances in physics, and the ability to discuss, argue and on occasions correct a theory with its originator. Furthermore unlike most 19th century scientists his interests embraced the philosophical issues raised by science. This and his quiet but sincere religious faith he shared throughout his life with the younger man. Hugh, Jemima and James remained friends until his death in 1879, though a certain cooling in their relationship is obvious after Clerk-Maxwell's marriage. His wife, Katherine Dewar, was looked upon with disapproval by the family. She was seven years older than he, and certainly in later life appears to have been decidedly neurotic. However, as Ivan Tolstoy in his perceptive study of Clerk-Maxwell says: 'he married a woman who, very likely, would neither disturb his work or his [religious] views.'

ON THE FIRST of September 1842 Queen Victoria began her first visit to Scotland. The monarch nearly took the citizens of Edinburgh by surprise as her yacht reached the east side of Granton pier as early as 8.30 in the morning. A signal flag that was to have flown from Nelson's Column on Calton Hill failed to appear, and the only indication that the Queen had arrived was a twin gun signal fired from the castle on the instructions of the Duke of Buccleuch. As no-one was expecting such a signal it seems only to have puzzled everyone who heard it. The Royal Party drove from Granton to Inverleith Row, then by Dundas Street (thus passing the end of Heriot Row), Hanover Street, Princes Street, Waterloo Place, and so down to Holyrood House, with crowds lining the whole route. Excitement was at such a pitch in the capital that it was thought safer for the Queen to stay at Dalkeith, some eight miles south of Edinburgh. Four days later Jemima, wearing a new light blue dress, was presented to the Queen by her mother, Jean Blackburn also being presented by Lady Clerk.

For some years before the Queen's visit, tensions had been visible in the Church of Scotland. It was strictly governed by statute and had no powers beyond those specifically granted by Parliament. This, coupled with fears of Catholicism increasing its influence through the government's inept handling of religious affairs in Ireland, and the problem of lay patronage, led to a breakaway group forming under the leadership of the impetuous but eloquent Thomas Chalmers. Events came to a head during the General Assembly of 1843 when Chalmers led his supporters out of a meeting in St Andrew's Church and established the Free Church of Scotland. Jemima, sitting high on Calton Hill with an unobstructed view along George Street, witnessed the walkout, and as always had her sketch book handy.

The Wedderburns, being Episcopalians, were not affected in any immediate way by the Disruption; though they took an active interest in the debates which rolled round Edinburgh, life for them continued in much the same way as it had before. Andrew wrote home frequently, his letters being passed round the family. His journey East had been leisurely. He spent some weeks in Egypt, and wrote vividly of its wonders. On reaching India he commissioned several small paintings from Jemima for his 'Tough Book'—Jemima as a child had been nicknamed Little Toughie and he had carried it on as his own affectionate name for her. He also wrote a number of Indian fables which she illustrated. These are in a tiny sketch book, and it is possible that they sent it back and forth between Edinburgh and Madras.

9 × 12.7 cm. Watercolour. Jemima painting in her garret at the top of 31 Heriot Row, her mother holding the dog for its portrait.

During the winter months Mrs Wedderburn and Jemima did not stray far from Edinburgh. Jemima went riding, sometimes with her brother and sometimes with a riding class she attended. Occasionally she and her mother would go to the theatre in the evening. More usually they sat at home, often in Jemima's 'garret', a small room at the top of the house that was easy to keep warm. Mrs Wedderburn would sew or read while her daughter painted. Jemima had always kept pets—dogs, cats, pigeons, and for a while two owls. The present favourite was a crow, Beelzebub. He seems to have been a character, and appears in many sketches, usually up to mischief. In the summer Mrs Wedderburn, Jemima and Beelzebub left 'auld 31' in George's care, and became itinerants, staying for weeks at a time at Killearn, Penicuik, St Mary's Isle and Glenlair.

Jemima was exceedingly fond of her uncle John, and enjoyed young James's company. Together they went 'tubbing' (a term they applied to sailing in half a barrel), walked, climbed, and went on various excursions. In August and September the various houses in the area would take it in turns to host archery meetings. These were a great social event, and the following notice appeared in one of the local papers after one such competition:

> The Toxophilite Club of the Valley of Urr held their last meeting for the season on Mrs. Lawrie of Ernespie's barn, on Tuesday the 12th curt. The club consists of from forty to fifty members.
>
> Their meetings this summer have been quite charming. They ranged over the whole valley, on this fair lawn to-day, and on that the next; and after their couple of hours of archery was over, a picnic took place on the spot. 'God save the Queen' was invariably sung with the most graceful loyalty; and the hospitable mansion adjoining gave them music and a hall for the evening quadrille, which wound up the delights of the day . . . .

Nor lacks the club its Laureate and its Painter to glorify the pastime. A scion of the House of Middlebie has lent gallantly to the archers his spirited songs; and a fair lady, a friend of the same house, has painted a couple of pieces.... The former picture represents William Tell aiming at the apple on his son's head; the latter, the chaste huntress Diana piercing a stag. Both are 'beautiful exceedingly'.

Jemima was amused enough by her cousin's song, a parody of Scott beginning 'Toxophilite, the conflict's o'er', to copy it down and illustrate it with a sketch for her William Tell picture. What the paper's report does not reveal is that she also proved the best shot on this occasion.

At the beginning of November Jemima travelled once again to London, this time journeying by train, to stay with the Clerks in Park Street. Many of her previous acquaintanceships were renewed, for instance with Sydney Smith and Samuel Rogers; and to her immense pleasure, when her uncle, Sir George, happened to mention to the Duke of Wellington that she was staying, he insisted that she attend a ball he was giving and wrote her out an invitation card in his own hand. Her uncle also took her to Whitehall Gardens to meet Sir Robert Peel and to look at his collection of paintings, and introduced her to his political contemporaries, Lord Brougham and Lord Raglan.

James Colvile once again escorted her, and on one notable day toward the end of November took her to have tea with Landseer, who although only thirty two had been elected to the Royal Academy. He was very impressed by her drawings, declaring that in portraying animals he had nothing to teach her. He lent her some of his own drawings to copy, and made her a present of some of his childhood sketches. No lasting friendship existed between them, but Landseer was sufficiently impressed by her work, and felt he knew her well enough, to call unannounced with friends so that they too could be shown it. He also arranged for a series of six small watercolours that Jemima had painted, illustrating the story of Tom Thumb, to be presented to the Queen's children.

The few informal lessons that Landseer gave her constituted the only formal training she had received. Her aunt, Lady Selkirk, decided that if she was going to take painting seriously she should have lessons from Frederick Taylor, an artist who, it is said, 'excelled as a painter of elegant sporting scenes in watercolour.' Jemima was distinctly unimpressed, and the lessons did not last long, the visits she made to the studios of her friends Daniel Macnee and MacWhirter, Millais and Peter Graham probably being in the long run of more value to her.

William Makepeace Thackeray was, according to Carlyle, 'A big fellow, soul and body ... a big fierce weeping hungry man.' He and Jemima first met on her second visit to London in 1843, when he was beginning to achieve some recognition for his contributions to *Punch*, a publication that had been launched the previous year. Their friendship developed and extended until his death in 1863, despite her Aunt Colvile's for a time not approving, and seemingly stopping their meeting. In 1847 the publication of *Jane Eyre* under the pseudonym Currer Bell caused much excitement. It was widely rumoured to be the story of Thackeray and his children's governess. The mysterious author, whose sex was the subject for great debate, was said to be the latter, writing in retaliation to Thackeray's depiction of her as Becky Sharp, *Vanity Fair* then being two-thirds of the way through its monthly appearances. The rumour was fuelled the following year by the appearance in the second edition of a preface torridly fulsome in its praise of him. Perhaps understandably, Mrs Colvile did not approve of her niece being visited by a man who not only was at the centre of such rumours but also was known to have a wife incarcerated in a lunatic asylum in France.

Jemima did not return to Scotland until August 1844. Hugh Blackburn had meanwhile matriculated at Trinity College, Cambridge, in 1841, and studied for some time with the intention of going to the Bar. He met and became close friends with a young man of about his own age who was creating a name for himself by publishing a series of able and original papers in the *Cambridge Mathematical Journal*. This young man with whom he shared the same inquisitive nature and quiet sense of humour, was William Thomson, later Lord Kelvin, who became one of the greatest of applied scientists.

The mathematical tripos was considered to be the prime test of academic ability, and a high place gained in it marked a man down as destined to rise high in society. Thomson came second and Hugh fifth. In May the following year the Chair of Natural Philosophy at Glasgow University became vacant, and to his father's great delight (he was then Professor of Mathematics) William Thomson was appointed to the post. Hugh returned to a fellowship at Trinity.

Jemima was now twenty two, an age when most of her contemporaries were either married or thinking seriously about it. She had her suitors, but all, from her point of view, were unsuitable. Most of her time was spent working at her painting. She experimented with oil paint and added etching and lithography to her printmaking repertoire, and all the time she drew. John Clerk-Maxwell noted in a diary of December 1845: 'Walk with James and Jemima to Botanical Garden to inspect Palm trees—for her sketching for a picture.' She produced a fine series of engravings illustrating a fable, 'The Wild Huntsman', and F. Schenck of Edinburgh published a lithograph of a drawing she had done the previous year when attending a race meeting at Warwick. This seems to have been her first tentative step into the marketplace, and it is difficult to say how successful it was. The following year *Blackwood's Magazine* published an illustration, almost a cartoon, by her. It shows the reserve yeomanry exercising on Portobello beach. However, more drinking than exercising is taking place, and the print is entitled 'Would the regulars have behaved thus?'

She now had sufficient experience to produce an illustrated book of her own, and from surviving sketches it can be seen that she had been contemplating the idea for some time. Eventually she chose to illustrate two fairy tales, both retellings of traditional stories that must have been heard countless times round the Blackburns' fireside.

Fortunio and The White Cat were both published by William Blackwood in the early months of 1847. Jemima had worked on the lithographic plates herself—producing first highly detailed sepia ink sketches both of how the completed print would appear, and how she would have to draw the reversed image onto the stone. The illustrations for Fortunio are full of life but somewhat diffident in their execution; however by the time she came to work on The White Cat (it is my assumption that Fortunio was completed first) she was fully at ease with the medium and she let her imagination have full rein. Many of the interiors illustrated are decidedly Egyptian in character. Ever since her brother Andrew's letters cataloguing his adventures there the country had fascinated her, and the figures, animals and two-legged cats are full of life. Plate VI, showing the cats' hunting party, is witty, lively, and strikingly original, only (unusually) the drawing of the horse's right leg letting her down. Not surprisingly both books proved very popular and sold out quickly.

Amid much excitement Andrew returned from India on leave, bringing with him a multitude of gifts including, for Jemima, a monkey and a tiger skull. The monkey unfortunately does not seem to have lived for long. It had been five years since Andrew and Jemima had seen each other, and although they had corresponded at fortnightly intervals they now revelled in each other's company. Andrew told Jemima that he was thinking of marriage. He had met the daughter of a Dr James Keir who had, when younger, been doctor to the Czar of all the Russias and was descended from Rob Roy Macgregor's youngest son. His daughter Joanna was 'young, gentle and gay' and the perfect match for Andrew. She and Jemima became friends almost on their first meeting. In July Andrew and his sister drove to Auchindarroch, a friend's house near Lochgilphead, where

11 × 18 cm. Watercolour. Auchindarroch, 24 July 1847. Left to right: Alastair Campbell, Jemima, Alexander Campbell, Andrew Wedderburn, Julia Campbell, Archibald Campbell.

Joanna Keir joined them. The drawings and watercolours that Jemima executed over this period breathe with life and vigour, and are among the most colourful works she ever produced. It was a happy and contented group that returned to Edinburgh a week or two before the wedding in the Trinity Chapel on 14 September.

Jemima, who appears to have made something of a habit of going on other people's honeymoons, seems to have accompanied Andrew and Joanna to London, saw them off on the long journey to India and again, spent the winter and spring with the Clerks in London.

As we have heard, Jemima cared little for classical music. However, during the next few months she suddenly produced a number of paintings of chamber groups and, even more surprisingly, portraits of opera singers. There are two reasons for this. Firstly, the Clerk family were enthusiastic amateur musicians, and were in the habit of drafting into their ranks some of the leading instrumentalists of the day. Jemima could rarely turn down an opportunity to 'do' the portrait of a notable person—whatever their field. Her paintings of the Clerk family's musical evenings show the likes of Charles Hallé, John Ella, and Piatti, occasionally adopting a more minor role than they would have been used to. How often, one wonders, was John Ella asked to abandon his violin in favour of a triangle? The other reason for this sudden interest in music and musicians was her growing and deepening friendship with Hugh Blackburn. He was passionately fond of music, and Jemima began, in late 1848, to accompany him to concerts. September 1848 was a particularly rich month musically in Edinburgh. They attended recitals given by Grisi, Alboni, and Mario, and saw Jenny Lind in *Lucia di Lammermoor* and *La Sonnambula*. A few days later, at the beginning of October, Chopin gave a recital in the Hopetoun Rooms, and from what we know of Hugh's tastes it would seem extraordinary if he did not attend; but if Jemima accompanied him, then for once she left her sketchbook at home.

The growing of friendship into love is touchingly observed through Jemima's paintings. Over the years Hugh develops from being just another one of the Blackburn boys to become the central figure, and an increasingly handsome central figure at that. Jemima, who nearly always portrays herself in her pictures, is found to be spending less time with Helen or her sister Jean, and more time with Hugh, sitting beside him on picnics and in carriages, and whenever possible riding beside him. Hugh was a careful and cautious young man and would entertain few thoughts of marriage until such time as he had a job. In 1849, shortly after he had been awarded his M.A. at Cambridge, the Chair of Mathematics at Glasgow University became vacant on the death of William Thomson's father. William persuaded Hugh to become a candidate; and in the light of his high placing in the Cambridge tripos, his original work in mathematical science (in particular with a double-suspension pendulum—known as the Blackburn pendulum—which facilitated notable advances in experimental physics) and the fact that his chief rival refused to take the religious tests that were still compulsory in Scottish Universities, Hugh secured the post. Almost immediately he asked Jemima to marry him.

Detail
11 × 15.5 cm. 19 August 1850. Hugh
and Jemima watching a storm on the
shore of Ardmillan.

For Jemima it was the high point of what had already proved an
exciting year. In 1848 she had a painting accepted and hung in the
Royal Academy, entitled 'Phaeton'. Although it had evoked little critical comment and did not sell, she was encouraged to attempt her
largest work to date. She called it 'Plough Horses Startled by a Railway
Engine', and submitted it to the Academy of 1849. To her great delight
it also was hung.

Some years earlier she had formed a close friendship with a young
medical student, Henry Acland, who was staying with Dr Alison and
his wife, neighbours in Heriot Row. He had told her about, and almost
certainly introduced her to, his great friend John Ruskin, who with
the publication of the first volume of *Modern Painters* was establishing
himself as the premier art critic in the country. It seems that Jemima
wrote to him asking his opinion of her picture. His reply, a masterpiece
of constructive criticism, is worth reproducing in its entirety:

Prince near Boulogne
Monday 24 April [1849]

My Dear Miss Wedderburn,

I was released from printers demons' on Saturday afternoon,
and I write as soon as I can.

It often happens to me to be asked by painters to look at their
pictures. I never go, if I can help it; when I do, I say as many
civil things as I can, quickly and bow myself out. If I thought
you like people in general, I should do the same to you, now
especially, for my hand is tired with writing and my eyes with
touching etchings that have failed me: But you are a very extraordinary person, and I believe you will not quarrel with me for
treating you as if you had more sense than most. I have heard

that you don't like blame; but I don't care. Nobody does for that matter; but I don't believe that you cannot take it as well as any one else, and I should think you had so little of it that it would be an agreeable change, so I shall write exactly what I felt about your picture.

In the first place, I don't like an ELABORATE jest. No jest will bear the time necessary to paint it, unless it involves the portraiture of human character also, as with Wilkie, Hogarth, and Teniers. But there is not MUCH jest in a pair of horses frightened by a steam whistle—and the little that there is evaporates long before you have laid your first coat of colour. Your subject would have made a vignette for PUNCH, but is not fit for canvas, and even in PUNCH would have needed some word of fun to carry it off. Moreover, the jest is not even one which exhibits your animals: neither horses nor men are seen to advantage kicking. It is a MEAN expression of resistance.

In the second place, do not suppose that you can dispense with those ordinary occurrence of sublimity and beauty which have been the subject and food of painting from the earliest ages: there has been machinery in the world since the days of Cheops, if not of Asshur; and that machinery has been historically represented on works of art—as our railroads ought to be, if we built pyramids; but machinery never has been CHOSEN as a subject, nor can ever become an agreeable one. You may say you like it; I say your taste is MORBID and must be changed. There are certain licences of taste, beyond which no one may safely go. One person may legitimately like beef, and another mutton; but when my wife was a little girl and took to eating slate-pencil, her governess whipped her until she left off; and you ought to be whipped till you give up painting railroads. There is no ravishment in them.

But the strange thing is that you have not only chosen the ugliest subject you could get, but the ugliest possible conditions of it! There are sublimities about certain railroad phenomena—one is the bulk and length and weight of the carriages drawn—which you have lost by drawing only the engine. Another in the blackness, fire, and fury of the engine itself, which you have lost by painting it in broad daylight, and of the pastoral colour of bright green. Another in the length of the line—which you have lost by putting a bit of it only, straight across your picture; and another in the height of the embankments, which you have lost by putting them below you. Don't tell me you DREW IT AS IT WAS. A change of ten feet in your position might have given you a sublime subject. I don't know how without extreme ingenuity you could get into a position so universally bad; and as if not content with that, you must needs pull the reins of your horse exactly parallel with your rail, as if you were a bricklayer and were going to build over your picture—I am losing my temper—and must put up my things besides; for the coast of France enlarges. I have a great deal more to say yet.

(Champagnole, Jura, Saturday evening)

You will say I have taken my time to recover my temper, but I have been on French roads ever since, and they are not calculated to calm one, any more than your grasshopper railroad. Where was I? On the tight rope, I see—and I have not done with the rail, neither: but what I have to say next is apropos of colour.

It does not seem to me that it is enough understood that colour can not be indifferent; it must be either thoroughly good and right, or it is a blemish. There are many subjects which do not want colour at all, and of those which are the better for it, none are bettered unless it be very good: hundreds of painters spoil their thoughts by painting them; they might be beautiful draughtsmen, but they ruin all by putting on bad colour: and they forget that colour is the most trite and commonplace TRUISM of art unless it be refined. I passed a French sign to-day: "A l'arbre VERT". The word "vert" adds marvellous little to the idea of the tree; and the green paint adds just as little to the drawing of it—unless the green be PRECIOUS as colour.

Now, I am not sure whether I can tell you what I mean by preciousness in colour;—I should have fancied from those rat's paws that I saw of your drawing, that your eye for colour was exquisite; and yet if I had seen this picture for the first example of your work, I should have said you had no eye for colour at all, and would never paint. Whether you have or have not, I cannot yet tell: this only I can tell you, that the colours of the landscape in that painting are WRONG, not merely cold and lifeless, but discordant. They would produce on the eye of a good colourist actual suffering, like that which singing out of tune would cause to a musician; and exactly as the musician would wish the person who sang to speak plainly, so the colourist would wish you to leave colour alone, and DRAW only. Still, those rat's paws make me think you have it in you, but you will have to work hard to get at it, even to get the SENSE of what is right. If you will go to the National Gallery and look at the picture of Van Eyck [Jean Arnolfini and his wife] you will see in the woman's gown what I mean by PRECIOUS colour, in green, and if you will copy carefully (ladies go—do they not?—to the National Gallery to copy) Titian's Bacchus and Ariadne, I think the light will come upon you all at once: I doubt if you will get it by going on from nature, and I cannot show you what I mean unless I could have a talk with you; only pray recollect this, that PAINTING is not squeezing the colour you want on your palette, and laying it on point-blank, blue when you want blue, and yellow when you want yellow. Colour is not to be got so cheaply; anybody could paint if that were all. Good colour is to be got only by a series of PROCESSES; deliberate, careful and skilful. Suppose you want a clear green, for instance; you must lay a ground; first of pure white—that goes over all your picture; then if you want your green deep and full, I believe

Overleaf
22.8 × 28.2 cm. Watercolour. 'The Highland Shoemaker.' Glenuig, Loch Ailort.

the best practice is to lay a coat of RED solidly first—perhaps two or three processes being needed to get this red what you want. That being ready to dry and fix, you strike over it the green with as few strokes as possible, so as to run no chance of disturbing the under colour. For another kind of green you lay white first; then yellow, pure upon the lights, and subdued upon the shadows; then you glaze the whole with transparent blue; and so on, there being different processes for every kind and quality of colour—all this requiring the greatest skill and patience and foreknowledge of what you have to do—you having often to bear to see your picture white where it is to be yellow, and brown where it is to be grey, and red where it is to be green, and blue where it is to be purple, and so on. Of all this—which is the ART—you seem to me to have no idea; you go straight at it, as a monkey would (and with something of the same love of mischief, I think): many artists: so called, of the day, do it too, and many of them draw cleverly with their heavy colour; but they are not Painters, though they think themselves so; they can't PAINT—they can merely draw and daub. I only know three PAINTERS in the Royal Academy—Mulready, Etty and Turner. Of these, Etty hardly ever does more than sketch, though he sketches the right way. Turner has methods of his own, suited for his own purpose, and for nobody else's. Mulready has got some awkward crotchets about using his colour THIN on the lights and letting the white come through, and often spoils his work by treating it like watercolour and stippling; but he is still the best guide you can have, if you have influence with him to make him frank with you. If he says you paint well at present, he is flattering and treating you like a girl; tell him so, and make him speak out, and he will teach you marvellous things.

Now, I have a good deal more to say to you—(as I shall not fill my paper, I needn't write across this sheet)—but I shall be travelling (I hope) tomorrow, and busy next day; and it is time you should have this, in case you are beginning another picture: so I will merely tell you that I thought your birds, one and all, quite delicious, and better in mere PAINTING than the rest of the picture; and I was much struck by the thoughtfulness of the whole.—but you must feel as well as think, and be unhappy when you see gentlemen doing nothing but smoke and lean over a railroad bridge, with fancy dogs. As I said before, that is all very well for PUNCH, but it is not fit to be painted seriously. You are capable of great things; do not affect the Byronic mélange. I believe that in him it was affectation—not conscious affectation, but actual affectation never the less—and if you mean to do anything really good or great, do not condescend to the meanly ludicrous. I think you might paint Dante if you chose; don't paint Dickens. Cultivate your taste for the horrible and chasten it: I am not sure whether you have taste for the beautiful—I strongly doubt it—but you can always avoid what is paltry; your strong love of truth may make you (as a painter) a kind of Crabbe, something disagreeable perhaps at times, but always majestic and powerful, so only that you keep serious, but if you yield to your love of fun it will lower you to a laborious caricaturist. I haven't time to be modest and polite, nor to tell you how much I respect your talent, nor how glad I should be if I COULD do anything like what is in your power: I can DO nothing, but I have thought about art, and watched artists, more than most people, and I am quite sure that I am right in the main respecting what I have told you; and when I come back to London, if I can have some nice quiet talk with you, or if you will come and draw with me and help me, as you kindly said you would, I think I may perhaps be able to set some of these matters in stronger light for you. Meantime accept my best wishes for your FAR advance in the art you love and believe me ever, faithfully and respectfully yours,

J. Ruskin

It is hard, now, to realise how important Ruskin was in Victorian society. After the death of Wellington in 1852 he could claim to have been the best recognised man in Europe. From Wordsworth to Proust there was hardly a distinguished man of letters who did not speak well of him, nor was his reputation confined to the arts: Bernard Shaw and Gandhi considered him to be one of the great social reformers, and his writings on economics led indirectly to the foundation of the Labour Party. As a critic his opinions were held in the same awe as those of New York theatre critics of the present day who can with a poor review close a show on Broadway overnight.

One wonders how Jemima reacted to his letter. It seems likely that she had already met him (he at least had seen her work), and that therefore she was able to read between the lines and find it really rather encouraging. Then again she may have found his criticisms well founded. Certainly she never painted much in oils, but as we shall see circumstances militated against this; nor for the next twenty years did she attempt anything on quite the same scale. What she cannot have known at the time was that the general air of irritability in the first part of his letter was caused as much by illness as it was by critical judgement, for he wrote in his diary for that day, 'Crossed to Boulogne, with desperate cold in head coming on, wrote half letter to Miss Wedderburn in carriage going over,.

Hugh and Jemima were married in St John's Chapel, Edinburgh, on 12 June 1849, and immediately afterward set out for Dalquhourn, a fine mansion on the banks of the Girvan Water in Ayrshire, that Hugh's mother had rented for the summer. Even on this most exciting of days Jemima found time to paint a small watercolour of herself and Hugh sitting in the garden relaxing, smoking, and enjoying the last of the evening sun. After spending two or three days in Ayrshire they travelled south to London, Paris, Lyons and Geneva, from there commencing a walking tour of the Swiss Alps.

From the beginning their marriage was a delightful success and, unusually for the time, not in the least intellectually stifling. Hugh's

Above and opposite
13.8 × 22 cm each. Ink. Life in the High
Street of Glasgow. These drawings
formed the basis of a set of prints
which were produced in 1852–3.

interest in mathematics lay not in its pure form but as a means of
explaining the natural world. He was a keen botanist, a knowledgeable
marine biologist, and a competent geologist and ornithologist, all
interest which complemented Jemima's own skills. For her own part,
while perhaps not fully understanding the mathematical aspects of
natural philosophy discussed by Hugh and his colleagues, she understood and was fascinated by its wider principles and was always gratified when her drawings could be used to demonstrate, illustrate or
even prove a scientific argument. From an early date the scientific
community regarded her work as accurate and truthful. Shortly after
their return from their honeymoon Professor James Forbes, the
author of the definitive book on the viscosity of glaciers, called to
study her paintings in order to determine how the glaciers had
changed since his last visit to Switzerland.

On their return they stayed at Drumshang, a farmhouse on the
Ayrshire coast, for a few weeks in order to enable Hugh to prepare
his first lectures. Then at the start of the academic year they moved
into rooms at No. 13 in the Old College of Glasgow University.
Hugh's quiet, reticent and undemonstrative disposition did not make
him a particularly good lecturer, and he never stirred anything
approaching enthusiasm in his classes, but the solid grounding that
he gave his students meant that before long he was held in high esteem.

Jemima did not like Glasgow. To someone brought up in the classi-
cally proportioned New Town of Edinburgh, Old Glasgow provided
something of a culture shock. The University was old and imposing,
and when seen from the street gave the appearance of a long row
of monastic-looking buildings with a fine stone balcony in front. An
archway led to three inner courts in the first of which stood a fine

and much admired staircase. Some years earlier many of the older parts of the buildings had been demolished and replaced with others wholly foreign to the original style. All the buildings were damp, uncomfortable, and totally unsuited to their purpose. The College stood on the High Street, the former backbone of the old city, and a part which was little changed from medieval times. During this period Glasgow had the worst urban deprivation and poverty in Britain, with the Saltmarket (a continuation of the High Street) being arguably the worst slum in Europe. Disease was rife and the cholera epidemic of 1848 had caused many deaths. Edinburgh's Old Town was little better but because of the geographical location of the capital's New Town Jemima had not had to live in close proximity to such disturbing scenes. To add to the novelty of her situation, she discovered she was pregnant.

With some relief the Blackburns escaped from Glasgow at Christmas and travelled to Kirkcudbright to spend a few days with Jemima's Aunt Selkirk. Around this time they made the conscious decision to spend as little time in the city as possible, and on their return Hugh set about renting Ardmillan, a mansion on the Ayrshire coast some three miles south of Girvan. It was ideally situated for their purposes, being well and truly in the country, and yet within convenient travelling distance from Glasgow.

Jemima gave birth to a son in the College rooms on 23 March 1850, and after much discussion he was named after his godfather, William Thomson, and was baptised in Jemima's old family church, St John's, in Edinburgh. A few weeks later at the end of term the family packed and departed for Ardmillan. The house turned out to be large, damp and not particularly comfortable. It sat close to the sea, commanding

14 × 23 cm. 28 December 1868. Riding
near the harbour,
Kirkcudbright—evening.

Detail
7.5 × 16.3 cm. Watercolour. 3 August
1851. William Thomson (later Lord
Kelvin) 'teaching projection' to
William Blackburn.

fine views across to the Isle of Arran and Ailsa Craig. After Glasgow
it seemed idyllic. Like most Victorian middle class families the Blackburns employed a nurse to help look after William. Unusually, however, her duties seem to have been confined to 'baby sitting' when
Hugh and Jemima undertook long country walks, Jemima preferring
to undertake the nursing of her child herself.

All summer an almost constant stream of visitors called at Ardmillan (mostly family wishing to see young William). None were more
welcome than William Thomson, who arrived early September
announcing that he planned to stay until a mutual friend, the
mathematician Archibald Smith, should call for him toward the end
of the month in his yacht the *Raven*. He and Hugh spent hours work-

Above. Detail
14 × 15.5 cm. Watercolour. William Thomson (Lord Kelvin) and Hugh working in the garden at Ardmillan. In the background is young William with his nurse; Jemima is painting sunflowers.

Detail
17.5 × 12.5 cm. Watercolour. 19 October 1850. Jemima and Hugh watching a spectacular display of the Northern Lights from the front of Ardmillan House.

16.2 × 5.3 cm. Watercolour. 7 December 1850. Riding through industrial Glasgow. Left to right: Miss Cowpar, G. Stirling, Jemima, C. J. Cowpar, Prof. Forbes, William Thornton.

ing in the garden under the shade of a tree while Jemima painted. Several days were spent picking fruit in the orchard, and in the evenings they walked along the shore by moonlight. The year drew inexorably on, and as the start of the university term came closer plans were made for the return to Glasgow. This they put off until the last possible moment, Hugh returning some days in advance to prepare No. 13 College, and to undertake various professorial duties. Toward the middle of October he returned to Ardmillan for Jemima and William. A magnificent display of the aurora borealis signalled the approaching winter and appropriately brought down the curtain on an Elysian summer.

Autumn and winter in the industrial cities of Britain during the Victorian age were unpleasant and unhealthy. Smoke and smog hung everywhere. Jemima painted a watercolour showing herself and a party including William Thomson and Professor Forbes riding through an industrial landscape that is almost Dantesque, the leading riders disappearing into the gloom, and the flares from distant blast furnaces showing only dimly through the fog. It does show, however, that she was now prepared to venture away from the University and was starting to enjoy a social life of her own. They entertained within the precincts of the College, and were in turn invited to dinner by several acquaintances. They attended the theatre, most notably to see Fanny Kemble and John Parry. Jemima chaperoned William Thomson, Professor Rankine, and Charles Mansfield a young man who had been at university with Hugh, to dances in the town.

During the winter Thomson and the Blackburns planned a trip

Detail
18.3 × 20.3 cm. Watercolour. June 1868.
Shooting young hoodie crows.

to be too small to travel, but old enough to be left in the care of his nurse and grandmother. As soon as the term ended they departed for London, where they spent a couple of days visiting friends and relations and making the almost compulsory visit to the zoo. Then, crossing the Channel, they spent eight days travelling by carriage through Lyons, Marseilles and Nice, eventually arriving at Mentone.

They travelled widely, enjoying and sharing each other's enthusiasms, Hugh patiently waiting while Jemima finished a sketch, she enthusiastically helping him search for botanical specimens; and on one occasion, in Genoa, he even persuaded her to accompany him to the opera. Thomson, who had travelled out by sea, met up with them in Pisa where they stayed for a week to enable him to attend to some work in the University. Shortly before their departure from Glasgow the Blackburns had been reading John Ruskin's recently published *Seven Lamps of Architecture*, and they must have been

impressed with it for their Italian tour takes in nearly every place mentioned, Jemima making sketches of several details on which Ruskin specifically comments. They spent a fortnight in Florence studying the paintings in the Uffizi and the medieval architecture of the city, which they found infinitely preferable to the medieval architecture of Glasgow, before moving on to Bologna, Padua and Venice, returning to Scotland, via Switzerland, at the end of July. The remainder of the summer they spent at Ardmillan.

The return to Glasgow in the autumn once again quenched Jemima's desire to paint. She had produced ninety watercolours and drawings in the five months from May until September (seventy four in the sixty three days they were touring in Italy), but in the following five months painted only five small pictures. It is hard to explain this dearth of work from Glasgow. It is possible that during the winter months she worked on oil paintings or at the various forms of print making with which she was conversant, and that these works have been lost or have not survived; and possibly her social duties did not give her time to paint. More likely though, was that she did not find Glasgow, and in particular industrial Glasgow, conducive to her style of painting. One watercolour sketch, perhaps significantly, shows her leaving Glasgow in a hansom cab, as if this event was in itself worthy of record. On rare occasions aspects of heavy industry did appeal to her aesthetic senses and then, despite Ruskin's dire warnings about machinery never being a suitable subject for painting, she would tackle it with vigour. In early March 1852 she accompanied William Thomson to Dupson's works to see a new steam hammer in operation. The noise, size and colours were awesome, and she had little difficulty in conveying the scene on the small 5 by 7 pad she carried with her.

By March she was expecting her second child, and was delighted to return to Ardmillan at the earliest opportunity.

Summer in Ayrshire now fell into a regular pattern. When the weather permitted they would drive or walk in the country, or swim in the sea; visitors constantly arrived and departed; Jemima painted and Hugh busied himself with multifarious projects. He had invested in a new camera, and once again the science of photography occupied much of his time. There is evidence suggesting that they experimented in combining painting and photography by using a projected negative for Jemima to work over, but the results were unsatisfactory. It was still necessary to pose for a photograph and therefore the resulting drawing was also stiff, formal and very unlike the lithe and vibrant figures she drew free-hand.

Toward the middle of September Mrs Wedderburn arrived from Edinburgh to supervise the running of the household over the period of the birth of her next grandchild. Margaret was born on 28 September (exactly a fortnight after the country had mourned the death of the Duke of Wellington). She was baptised, after the family's return to Glasgow, in St Mary's Episcopal Church.

Glasgow was enduring yet another outbreak of cholera, not as severe as that of 1848–9, but still taking a heavy toll of life. Jemima at last brought herself, or was persuaded, to portray life in the streets

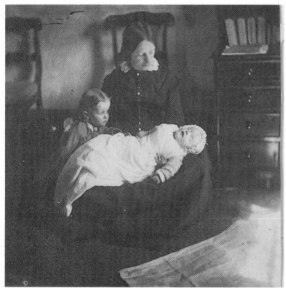

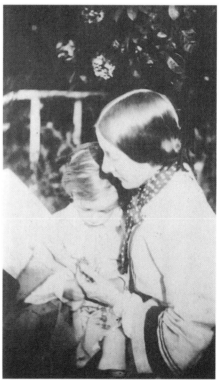

9.8 × 6.2 cm. Albumen print. Jemima and William photographed by Hugh (1853).

5.5 × 4.5 cm. Albumen print. Jemima and Doll at the back door of Ardmillan House. Photographed by Hugh on or around 9 July 1852.

surrounding the College. She drew a series of pencil studies, later engraved, showing the deprivation, squalor, drunkenness and fighting frequently to be seen in the High Street directly outside the College gate.

In early 1851 she had attended a sermon in Edinburgh given by the prominent Free Churchman, Dr Thomas Guthrie, who was to become known as the 'apostle of the Ragged School movement'. His eloquence and his message stirred the public's conscience, and in spite of the bigotry he displayed in not allowing Roman Catholic teaching in his schools (many of the children being Irish Catholics) he helped greatly to end the iniquity of delinquent children simply being imprisoned. With the contrast of her own happy and contented family thrown into sharp relief by the scenes she witnessed every day in the High Street, it was clear that her conscience would lead her to do something to help. She decided that she would illustrate a book which could be sold on behalf of the Glasgow Ragged School, her previous publications being successful enough to indicate that this was no empty gesture, but indeed one which should bring the movement a substantial sum of money. She chose to illustrate Susannah Moodie Strickland's *The History of Little Downey*, which, as it was first published in 1822, was probably a favourite in the nursery when Jemima herself was a child. Hugh suggested an original method of reproducing her illustrations, utilising photography. She etched her drawings onto a piece of glass which had been covered with a thin opaque coating. When this was placed on a piece of light-sensitive paper and exposed to a light source, the drawing would be reproduced in a black line. By this means a large number of identical plates could be produced. (There is ambiguous evidence to suggest that they may have experimented with this procedure some twelve years earlier.) Hugh seems to have been able to manipulate the process to produce a wide range of graphic effects, from that of a line engraving to the soft look of a tinted lithograph. The frontispiece he produced conventionally from a paper negative, a method he found 'more troublesome and tedious than either of the other [methods] both in preparation of negative and in printing'. All the work on the book they carried out in the College rooms, though it is possible that Constable and Co. of Edinburgh undertook the binding, and it was certainly through them that it was distributed. No copy of this publication has been traced, and it is probable that once again Hugh's desire to experiment led to the end product being unstable in light.

Jemima's skill as an illustrator was becoming more widely recognised, and in early 1853 she was commissioned to produce a frontispiece for a book called *Louisa von Plettenhaus or ; the journal of a young lady*, and a series of etchings to illustrate *Lorenzo Benoni or ; passages in the life of an Italian*. Both books were published by Constable, and of the latter *Bell's Messenger* stated that it 'should be as extensively read as *Uncle Tom's Cabin*', *The Scotsman* of 31 December complimenting its 'neat portable shape illustrated with graceful etchings'.

DURING 1848, 'the year of revolutions' at the end of the previous decade, a group of young men had met at 83 Gower Street in London to form a secret society. Like many another group at the time they wished to overthrow the establishment. However, unlike most of the others, they had little interest in the confused politics of the day. They were young poets and painters who, inspired by Ruskin's clarion call in *Modern Painters*: 'Go to nature in all singleness of heart, selecting nothing, rejecting nothing', set out to break the virtual monopoly the Royal Academy had on the public's aesthetic sensibilities. The movement they spawned, Pre-Raphaelitism, was to act as the medium for the Romantic spirit of the century, becoming a strange reforming phantom which drifted through Victorian life affecting everything that came into contact with it, from literature, art and design to religion and politics. It was a complex movement that even its originators did not understand fully: an escape from industrial society and yet at the same time a means of changing it.

During a short stay in London before moving to Ardmillan for the summer, John Ruskin introduced Jemima to John Everett Millais, one of the founders of the Pre-Raphaelite Brotherhood. The hostility that his paintings had initially aroused had, by 1853, given way to almost universal praise. Although they never became close friends, Jemima and Millais kept in contact over the years, both being prepared to cast a critical eye over the other's work. The philosophy behind the Pre-Raphaelite movement had a profound influence on Jemima, and from the date of their first meeting several changes can be found in her work, both in design and technique.

The Blackburns, Millais, John and his wife, Effie Ruskin, all left London for Scotland at the end of June, Hugh and Jemima heading for Ardmillan, Millais and the Ruskins planning on spending a month or so in the Trossachs, ostensibly for Millais to paint Ruskin's portrait. Ruskin was a quiet unemotional man who preferred the study of inanimate objects to the pleasures of society. He had an almost boyish notion of femininity, and when confronted with the real thing had recoiled in horror. Effie, an attractive and spirited girl who loved society, had endured his inattentions for six years, and when she found herself courted by the young, handsome and immensely talented Millais, inevitably fell in love with him. The following year she instituted proceedings for the annulment of her marriage on the grounds that it had not been consummated, and a year later married Millais. Needless to say Victorian society revelled in the drama, and even among those who knew the participants well the occasional social *faux pas* could arise. Hugh admitted in a footnote to Jemima's memoirs that ever after he found difficulty in not referring to Mrs Millais as Mrs Ruskin.

For some time the Blackburns had desired a home that they could call their own, and now, in the summer of 1853, they decided to search in earnest. On returning to Ardmillan from London they paused for barely a week before sailing across the Firth of Clyde to the Mull of Kintyre to commence the search. Both had considerable experience in the procedure, having helped Hugh's elder brother, Colin, to search

Detail
15.2 × 20.1 cm. In the portion of Jezreel shall Dogs eat the flesh of Jezebel. From *Illustrations from Scripture by an Animal Painter*, published by Thomas Constable and Company (1854–5). This example taken from the later edition, *Bible Beasts and Birds*, Keegan Paul and Trench (1886).

for and eventually purchase the estate of Doonholm. Jemima relates their adventures in her memoirs, and produced a remarkable small sketchbook detailing their travels in an amusing and almost comic book manner. They travelled as far north as Loch Coruisk in Skye—virtually a must on any traveller's schedule since the days of Turner and Scott—but returned at the end of August having seen nothing that would suit their purpose.

It was probably around this period that Jemima began work on her first major publication. Showing sound commercial judgement she decided to combine two categories in which books at that time always sold well, namely animal illustration and the Bible. *Illustrations from Scripture by an Animal Painter*, as she decided to entitle the work, consists quite simply of illustrations of those scenes in the Bible in which animals appear. A few of the illustrations are weak in design, drawing and conception, and I think it is reasonable to assume that these constitute her first tentative steps into the project; but as her confidence grew she began to produce some extraordinary original illustrations. With the Pre-Raphaelite credo of 'truth to nature' in mind, she drew only what she knew, setting many of her drawings in the Ayrshire landscape, and for others working up sketches made when touring abroad. She used friends and family as models, Hugh and William appearing together as Abraham and Isaac. Once again she chose to use photography as a means of reproduction, and for this reason worked on a scale somewhat larger than usual. Unfortunately this meant that when the plates were reduced in size during printing they lost much of their spontaneity.

For reasons which have been lost in the mists of time the Blackburns referred to their 'dream house' as 'Dimity', the search for which was resumed the following summer. A journey to Ardnamurchan produced little of interest, though they were told about a property which lay in an isolated corner of the peninsula known as Moidart. Their attempts to view the estate were frustrated by the weather, and eventually they were forced to return to Ardmillan. During the autumn a further attempt was made, and to their delight they discovered that

Detail
5 × 20.5 cm. Watercolour. 28 September
1854. Margaret's second birthday party
which took place the day after the estate
of Roshven had been purchased. Left to
right: Alice Mackenzie, Doll, Margaret,
Barbara MacFee, Jemima, Hugh and
William.

it was the 'beautiful place' they had felt sure must lie round the corner
when on a tour of the Highlands twelve years earlier, they had stood
on the shore at Kinlochailort and debated what lay at the mouth of
the loch. Hugh, on his return south, immediately opened negotiations
for its purchase, and on 27 September 1854 the estate of Roshven
became theirs.

Margaret's birthday party the following day thus became a double
celebration. Everyone dressed up, even Hugh wearing a flamboyant
blue tie. In Jemima's drawing he seems somewhat preoccupied,
perhaps wondering what he had let himself in for with his purchase.
The house was in need of extensive renovation, and the only means
of getting building materials to the site would be by sea, for Moidart
was an extremely remote part of the western seaboard. Father Charles
MacDonald, writing in 1889, describes it as 'exceedingly savage and
rugged' with 'bold and romantic scenery'. It was chosen for its isola-
tion by Charles Edward Stuart when looking for a place to land on
the British mainland at the outset of the ill-fated '45 rising, and maintained its air of impregnability until recent times, a road through the
region being completed only in 1966 and mains electricity not arriving
until 1983.

Over the winter Hugh and Jemima had a lot of work to attend
to. In addition to his professorial duties, Hugh had undertaken to
edit and revise Sir George Airy's *Treatise on Trigonometry*, and
Jemima had books by an old acquaintance, the popular author
Charlotte Yonge, to illustrate.

Jemima's own reputation was growing. On 30 November 1853 Effie

17.6 × 25 cm. Watercolour. Harvesting
potatoes, Roshven.

Ruskin wrote to her friend Rawdon Brown that 'we . . . go to Mrs. Blackburn who is a great friend of John's and the best artist he knows . . . .' An exaggeration perhaps, but even so it is clear that he enjoyed her company, for he had recalled the occasion in a letter to Lady Trevelyan (9 January 1854): 'After I saw you at Perth I had a somewhat disagreeable round of confused visitations to pay at Glasgow . . . . I wasn't comfortable, in spite of the kindest efforts on the part of the kindest friends to make me so—except for some half day or so at Mrs. Blackburn's where I enjoyed myself particularly—but even then under a species of horror from the sense of neighbouring steam engines and forges and other disturbances.'

In December *Illustrations from Scripture by an Animal Painter with Notes by a Naturalist* was published. It achieved almost immediate widespread critical and popular success. Landseer wrote to the publishers, 'If any praise of mine can add to the popularity of this charming work, I have great pleasure in repeating my sincere admiration for its extreme originality of conception and admirable accuracy of knowledge of the creatures delineated. Having studied animals during my whole life, perhaps my testimony as to the truth of the artist's treatment of the Scripture Illustrations may have some influence.'

Thackeray wrote directly to Jemima:

36 Onslow Sqr Brompton   16 Feb [1855]

Dear Mrs. Blackburn,

Two days since, Millais and Phillips Portrait-painter and Leech were dining with me and the Scripture Animals were on the table.

These gentlemen said the drawings were the finest they had seen for ever so long a time; and two of them went off with an intention of buying the book straightway—sure the best compliment that artists can pay a sister artist.

Now is the time, thinks I, to write that note to Mrs. Blackburn—Mrs. Hugh Blackburn, which you owe her this ever so long a time—even she, living in a cloister, surrounded by the grave and wise, will not be displeased at hearing by what critics her genius is appreciated. The pictures grow upon me like all good things. I spy out little secrets unperceived before—why, it was not till last night I saw the little beak of the chick under the hen peering out from the beautiful fluffy white maternal feathers. I don't know whether I like that or the Owls or the Deluge or the Scapegoat best—I think the Swine running into the sea is a grand composition; and the Plague of Frogs—well, I must own that the plague of frogs made me laugh—especially that fellow jumping into the vase. The pretty little Egyptian ballet children are very quaint and pleasant to look at—and gourrawarrawow how those dogs are serving Jezebel right! Those vultures coming up are very fine and tragic. What a deal of pleasure you have given me!

The Times dined with me yesterday, and I urged upon him the necessity of enlightening the public respecting these drawings.

Not that I suppose the public will really care for them, and the dreadful fee of two guineas will operate as a barrier between you and popularity. I know I wouldn't sell MY copy for two guineas, though I got it at a considerable reduction! The cost of production was one of the questions I was going to ask you when I got the book first—a query answered by your note and the price put on the book.

I have been to Paris twice since I owed you this note—to visit my parents—to be ill—to fetch home my daughters—have had a very great deal to write and to do,—otherwise I should have written earlier to thank you for the great pleasure which you have given me and continue to give me. That boy must have the love of animals and the sportsman instinct strongly developed in him, to make such a remark as that about Jezebel's paint! I hope I shall know him some day and see more drawings in your portfolio.

Give my best regards to Lushington and to Thomson please with his nice wife; and pardon me for forgetting your husband's Xtian name. U and I (a neat and novel pun) are very different— you can draw and have worked and have done it. I ought to have could, and have been idle, and neglected that good gift. I always feel sad and ashamed when I think of this.

Ever yours, dear Mrs. Blackburn, Very sincerely,
W. M. Thackeray

Ruskin also wrote to congratulate her:

Dear Mrs. Blackburn,

I have your book and am much pleased with it. It is impressive and in many respects delightfully original. I like Jezebel better than I expected—only she needn't have had quite such a broad foot,—and I like Pharaoh—frowning at the sea—and I like the little girl who don't like frogs, and I like Lazarus (perhaps the best of all), and I like the ape talking to the peacock about his tail, and I like intensely the swallow and the stork. But how in the world could you poke the best beloved Ass into the stall with the ox? Of all the beasts she should have been first—you should have put her with her colt at the meeting of the two ways. And how in the world could you miss the SERPENT?

Bill with his sticks is delightful. I had not caught the idea of the crown of thorns. I wish you had written the illustrations yourself—you know the printer would have put the spelling to rights.

I CANNOT get you inventive people to explain your own notions in a plain way to the public.

I am writing something about the book. Would you ask your publisher—No—I'll manage it myself.

Ever faithfully yours,
J. Ruskin.

13.3 × 10.2 cm. The fate of the Black
Wolf, and Leonards Dream. Two
illustrations from *The Lanes of Lynwood*
by Charlotte Yonge, published by John
Parker and Son (1855).

The article he wrote appeared in the *Morning Chronicle* on 20 January 1855, and praised the artist's originality, life and sincerity.

Thackeray's fears that the price might deter the general public seem to have been unfounded, and the book sold well and steadily. It was republished during 1866 under the more concise title *Bible Beasts and Birds*. The silver prints in the original edition had proved to be unstable, and most copies had faded badly. The new edition used the original drawings, which were reproduced by the more permanent palinotype process. Two of the original illustrations were rejected as inferior, one being 'The Ox and Ass' which Ruskin had condemned; and four new plates were added. One of these had actually appeared in the earlier edition. Jemima scraped out and repainted the head of a figure, improving the drawing and adding a beard. She also changed the text in the same manner. Once again the book proved to be a tremendous popular success. Lady Eastlake praising its 'great charm of unconventionality'.

The Lances of Lynwood and *The History of Sir Thomas Thumb*, two of the books she had illustrated for Charlotte Yonge also sold well. They are both retellings of traditional tales, a form, as we have seen, that she particularly enjoyed illustrating. For *The Lances of Lynwood* she produced seven atmospheric, almost claustrophobic, engravings of unequal quality. Tom Thumb, however, brought out the best in her, and she made a series of highly inventive and curious woodcuts (engraved by Dalziel), very reminiscent of the strange, highly detailed fairy paintings that Richard Dadd was producing around the same time in Bethlem Lunatic Asylum. Surprisingly, they draw only marginally on the content of the earlier group of Tom Thumb paintings that Landseer had presented to the Queen's children.

During 1855 Jemima had also published a strange little book with the even stranger title of *Caw Caw*. She had first conceived the idea for this tale in verse during the years at Ardmillan. It relates the story of a year in the life of a group of crows from nesting in the spring to their demise at the hands of a group of farmers in the early summer.

> Now let us homeward go, they say,
> and gathering up their slaughtered prey
> His share each one in bundle ties
> and takes them home to make crow pies.

The *Morning Herald* reported that 'The illustrations are excessively droll, and no impartial crow could attempt to dispute the fidelity of the portraiture.' It proved to be a most popular publication, with the first edition speedily selling out. A second was issued containing a detail, showing a child reading the book, from one of the pictures by John Leech—'a spontaneous compliment from Mr. Leech which "Caw Caw" could not but gratefully acknowledge'.

In the 1850's steamers left Glasgow for Oban, Tobermory and Portree every Friday at eight o'clock, unless, as the timetable warned, prevented by some unforeseen occurrence. The steamer's captain could be persuaded to anchor in the deep water at the mouth of Loch Ailort, some half a mile off shore from Roshven House, and thus it was that on 15 May 1855 a flotilla of small boats ferried the Blackburns and their possessions ashore. The house sat on a flat raised piece of ground at the end of a long white sandy bay. Beyond, to the north east, a small bare hill gave the house some shelter from winter winds. Behind, a small wood of old and weatherbeaten oak trees soon gave way to the steep slopes of Rosbheinn (the mountain that lent its name to the estate) which rose to nearly three thousand feet. To the south west lay open, barren moorland stretching down to a rocky shore.

The days that followed were days of discovery and exploration. For the first time in six years of marriage they were able to spend the summer on their own. No visitors were intrepid enough to venture north, and it is perhaps surprising therefore to discover that Jemima completed under a dozen watercolours over the period, surprising only because of her usual prodigious output when visiting somewhere new. Under the circumstances, the only real wonder is that she found time to paint at all. Many things pleased, but others did not, and the list in Hugh's pocket book of matters to be attended to grew by the day. They decided very quickly that the house would have to undergo a fairly radical transformation before it was as they wished.

By the time the family returned to Glasgow in October Jemima was five months pregnant. Named after his father, Hugh was born on February 1856 in the College rooms, and a few days later baptised in St Mary's. He was a sickly child, and the first four months of his life were traumatic for his parents, the prevailing dampness in the College buildings and the filthy smog-filled city air not helping his condition at all. But his health improved dramatically when the family moved back to Roshven in May. The house had been made more comfortable than the previous year, but even so, when a party consisting mainly of the Professor's brothers and sisters arrived in July, it must have seemed very cramped. The kitchen was the focal point of the children's lives. It was here that 'Babby' ruled the roost. She was a large, comfortable cheery person who could manage to keep an eye on the children, tend to the hens, chickens, ducks, cats, and pet lambs that lived in or wandered into the kitchen, amuse young Hugh in his cradle, and prepare dinner for eight. The days passed slowly and leisurely. Professor Hugh worked on his masterplan for the estate. Not only did he plan to rebuild the house but he wished to extensively landscape the grounds around it. Like everything he undertook this was gone into with great deliberation and total thoroughness. Unlike many Victorian fathers he also spent a great deal of time with his children. They were often with him as he considered the future shape of the estate, and accompanied him on long walks on which he would frequently stop to show them flowers or birds' nests, or else he would spend hours with them investigating the rock pools along the seashore. Jemima, as always, painted, her work now achieving a fluidity, confidence and maturity that perhaps it had lacked before. After dinner, with the children in bed, they would often take a boat and go fishing in the bay in front of the house, watching the sun sink in a blaze of pink and orange behind the spectacular outline of the islands of Eigg and Rhum, then rowing back in the warm gathering dusk with baskets of mackerel for the morning's

13 × 22.5 cm. Watercolour. September
1856. 'An encounter with a whale,
Loch Ailort'.

breakfast. Occasionally these trips provided unexpected excitement.
On one occasion a whale surfaced uncomfortably close to the boat
from which they were fishing. Jemima recalled that it looked very
large when its great black back rose out of the water as it took breath
and spouted. 'It came rather nearer to our boat than the rowers quite
liked.'

In November and December 1856 Thackeray visited Glasgow to
deliver his lectures on 'The Four Georges'. He dined with the Blackburns on most evenings and did so again on a return visit the following
February. Glasgow provided a magnificent turnout for his lectures;
but though gratified by the numbers who wished to hear him, he was
upset by the organisers, who had booked the series for a set fee of
£100, based on calculations that he would lecture to not many more
than six hundred people. They however had hired the city hall with
room for an audience of three thousand, and thus boosted their profits
by an extra £500 to £600.

The following summer Jemima's brother Andrew, on one of his
rare periods of leave, brought their mother north to see the house

Sept 1856

and estate. To everyone's regret he was not able to stay, for the Indian Mutiny had broken out that May and Roshven was too isolated to receive news quickly. In July, when Jemima painted him on a family outing to one of the islands in Loch Ailort, reports of the massacre of soldiers, women and children at Cawnpore had reached London. He left shortly after, and dashed south, leaving Mrs. Wedderburn to spend the rest of the summer at Roshven.

James Clerk-Maxwell arrived to spend a few days in early September (apparently his only visit to Roshven). His father had died the previous year, a loss that he found 'incalculable and irreparable', and although he had thrown himself into a new appointment at Aberdeen University he was prone to fits of melacholy and, as he always seemd to do at moments of crisis in his life, expressed himself in verse:

> Alone on a hillside of heather,
> I lay with dark thoughts in my mind
> In the midst of the beautiful weather
> I was deaf, I was dumb, I was blind.

Although the hillside referred to is as likely to be at Glenlair as at

Roshven it is indicative of the state of mind he was in during his visit. He had never formed the same easy relationship with the Blackburn children that William Thomson managed, and though both Professor Hugh and Jemima enjoyed his company greatly, he perhaps found it difficult to fit into the Blackburn's family life. He appears in only one of Jemima's paintings during his visit, attending a dance held one evening on the lawn in front of the house. He is sitting watching with a sad distant expression. He returned south with Mrs. Wedderburn, and it is clear from a letter he wrote on his return to Glenlair just to what extent Roshven was cocooned from news of the outside world. 'I have just returned from the remote Highlands, and have met all the Indian news on the way', he wrote to R. B. Litchfield.

Three months before he had written to C. J. Monro (a friend from his student days): '. . . I saw a paragraph about the Female Artists Exhibition, and that Mrs. Hugh Blackburn had her 'Phaeton' there . . . . She has done a very small picture of a haystack making, somewhat pre-Raphaelite in pose, but graceful withal, and such that the Moidart natives know every lass on the stack, whether seen behind or before. It was at the Edinburgh Academy of Painters.'

The Female Artists Exhibition to which he refers seems to have been the first exhibition of the Society of Female Artists which was held at 315 Oxford Street from 1 June to 18 July 1857. The growth of this important and influential society—which still exists as the Society of Women Artists—is hard to follow as its archives were destroyed during the second world war. It had its inception in the desperate need for women artists to be able to exhibit in an atmosphere which did not discriminate against them. Even the term 'women artists' was a revolutionary one, it being thought that only men could be artists. The Royal Academy Schools did not admit female students and, although a campaign was mounted to change this, it was not until they admitted L. Herford, purely on merit, in 1861, and realised too late and with great embarrassment that the L stood for Laura, that this ceased to be the case. The Royal Academy, as we have seen, did admit paintings by women, but it was seemingly impossible for a critic to discuss their work on the same level or in the same terms as for men, nearly always preceding his comments with some condescending phrase along the lines of 'this fair hand' or 'an accomplished lady'.

Jemima not only painted in oils, often considered too smelly and dirty for women, but etched, engraved and printed her own plates, worked her own lithographic stones, cut and printed her own wood blocks, and also worked in the then *avant garde* medium of photography. She had always seen herself as a serious artist, but it is only with this entry in the S.F.A. exhibition that we see her publicly nailing her colours to the mast as a woman artist, the only sadness being that, at a time when she was painting some of her finest work, she should choose to show a picture that was nine years old.

In September 1857 the gallery owner and entrepreneur, Ernest Gambart, had a notion to send an exhibition of British paintings to America for what would be the first show of its kind. He was surprised

16 × 25.3 cm. Watercolour. 12 September 1857. A dance outside Roshven House on what seems to have been James Clerk-Maxwell's only visit to Moidart. Left to right: Barbara MacFee (Babs), young Hugh, Hugh, James Clerk-Maxwell, William, Margaret, Mrs Wedderburn, . . .?, . . .?, Jemima.

to discover that a certain Captain A. A. Ruxton had similar plans. Ruxton knew little about art, but, like so many others, knew what he liked. After some discussion the two schemes were combined and Ruxton was appointed manager. The influential magazine *Art Journal*, on hearing of the plan, believed it 'next to impossible to collect a sufficient number of high class pictures . . . and strongly advise[d] its postponement for a year.' This advice was ignored, and works by one hundred and seventy five painters—only twenty two being women—including Turner, Leighton, Holman Hunt, Maclise and Roberts were assembled. Jemima was asked to contribute, and had six pictures included. She was the only woman to show both an oil and watercolours, though once again the oil she chose to send was a work that had been completed some years before, entitled, with an astute eye on the American public, 'Scene on the coast of Ayrshire, near the birth place of Robert Burns'. The watercolours were of a more recent date, and included at least one painted at Roshven.

When the exhibition opened in New York on 19 October 1857 it coincided with one of the greatest financial disasters of the century, and from a commercial point of view was almost a complete failure.

19 × 20.3 cm. Watercolour. Building a haystack. Irine, Roshven. Possibly the watercolour referred to by James Clerk Maxwell in his letter to C. J. Munro.

The *New York Times* complained that 'Many of the best names in English Art are wholly unrepresented . . . [and] are hung without respect to . . . the laws of color—Pre-Raphaelite intensities "killing" naturalist composure and flagrant oils literally burning the life out of quiet aquarelles.' The *Crayon* magazine however was not so disparaging; '. . . the exhibition is pronounced universally to be exceedingly interesting and instructive. It combines far more excellence than is ever visible in any one exhibition of the Royal Academy, or than could be seen in any one collection of Modern Art in England.' The American public's outraged modesty necessitated the removal of two of Leighton's paintings, 'Pan' and 'Venus and Cupid', but, despite all the problems, there were successes. Holman Hunt's 'Light of the World' (a smaller version of the original) proved highly popular. The exhibition limped on to Philadelphia in February 1858 and by April had reached Boston, where it eventually closed.

IT IS APPROPRIATE to pause at this point, virtually half way through Jemima's career, and assess how she stood in relation to her contemporaries. She was as good a draughtswoman as any of the members of the S.F.A., and possessed a command of print-making that few, if any, of them could equal. Her watercolour technique may have been idiosyncratic but it was extremely versatile, and she had over the years picked up many curious technical tricks which she could use to stunning effect. Realising, however, that she lacked the technical expertise, particularly in oil painting, of a Rosa Bonheur, Henrietta Ward or Elizabeth Thomson Butler to challenge the male-dominated 'fine art' world, she seems to have decided upon a subtle change of direction and begun to paint less for public exhibition, and to concentrate even more on her illustrative work. This was a field where discrimination was no less evident, but was one where not only had she a proven record but one where she could compete on more equal terms. This did not indicate any withdrawal of support from those women pushing for equality within the art world, but more a realisation that her talents and her ambitions would be of more effect on the flanks rather than in the front line.

Except for this understandable interest in women's emancipation, she had little time for the politics of the art world, and even less for political painting. There was much controversy at the time, among the gallery-going public, as to the sociological context of paintings. In 1858 Henry Wallis exhibited in the Royal Academy one of the most poignant and enduring images of 19th century British painting. 'The Stonebreaker' showed a figure crouched amidst a desolate landscape of crushed stones and lit by a twilight of radiant beauty. It was seen as an obvious comment on the Poor Law, which turned the residents of the poorhouse to hard labour. Many critics found it outrageous. John Ruskin thought it the picture of the year. Jemima's early Academy picture, 'Plough Horses Startled by a Railway Engine', could be construed in a similar vein, but since then she had come to realise that such political content was, by its very nature, of its

Frontispiece to *The Instructive Picture Book*, seventh edition published by Edmonston and Douglas, Edinburgh (1866).

day, destined to be forgotten almost as quickly as the cause which inspired it. She would see it as curious and somewhat ironic that today we find the sociological aspects of her work so interesting. We do, only because she did not. She painted her family, the people of the West Highlands and of the countries she visited, purely as documentary records for her own, and her family's, private interest and enjoyment. They contained no message and recorded only what she saw. They were rarely intended for public exhibition, and the haystack-making picture referred to by Clerk-Maxwell seems to be a notable exception.

Around this period Jemima was asked to contribute an illustration or two to Adams White's *Instructive Picture Book*, a volume for children illustrating and describing aspects of natural history. The early editions contain only a few examples of her work, but her popularity seems to have been such that by the time it reached its seventh edition in 1866 she not only had designed its cover and frontispiece but contributed seventeen out of twenty seven pages of illustrations. In this latter format it is a delightful book, the plates lithographed with the outline, background and base colours, all the colouring of the animals, birds and flowers then added by hand. This resulted in a series of glowing and vibrant illustrations which breathe life. It gives a rare opportunity to compare her work, at the turn of a page, with that of other illustrators working in the same field, and it is immediately obvious that her drawings are less formalised and are more freely and naturally drawn than those of the other contributors, whose efforts would not seem out of place in a book of fifty years earlier.

The following year yet another book was published under the initials J.B., the monogram by which she was now identified, *Scenes of Animal Life and character from Nature and Recollection*. Once again it is primarily a children's picture book, originally appearing in two formats, either in black and white, or in colour. In it she collates a number of sketches made over the previous ten years, entitling them humorously in groups, 'The St. Bernard dog—romance and reality', 'Fox hunting—in sport and earnest', etc. They contain several enchanting examples of her sense of humour.

Dr John Brown wrote the archetypal Victorian moralistic animal story *Rab and his Friends* in 1859, and during 1861 was planning an illustrated edition. He wrote to Lady Trevelyan, asking her to contribute an illustration, and continued, 'I want Noel Paton to do the dead old woman in bed and Mrs B, Rab keeping guard at the foot of the bed and the room very dark and perhaps my foot seen to show somebody else—but merely the foot. Then I am for George Harvey ... William Hunt .... Then I want Mrs B to do a Carrier's cart from life ... and the hen coop at the back of the cart with the inquisitive and doomed fowls poking out. This would suit her desperately realistic turn ....'

These publications were popular and successful but lightweight in character. Her next project was to be quite different. She had always been interested in birds, even keeping a pigeon in her doll's house when she was a child. Heriot Row had also housed at various times

Detail
25 × 26.5 cm. Sepia Ink. 12 June 1872.
Jemima drawing eagle chicks above
Loch Ailort.

parrots, macaws, canaries, Beelzebub the crow, and two owls which
came to an unfortunate end when they were killed by the Earl of
Selkirk's dogs when he stayed overnight en route to the grouse moors
of Perthshire. In more recent years she had kept a heron, captured
at Killearn, in the bathroom in the College rooms, and had fed it
sardines whilst its portrait was being painted. Her ornithological
studies had been long admired. Even Ruskin had singled out the birds
as virtually the sole point of merit in 'Plough Horses Startled by a
Railway Engine', and by 1860 she was beginning to plan their
publication.

'Works on Birds of the World are innumerable', grumbled John
James Audubon in 1836. His extraordinary *Birds of America* had been
immensely costly to produce and, due to a strike by the colourists,
had taken twelve years to complete. Prideux John Selby's *Illustrations
of British Ornithology* (1821–34) were somewhat overshadowed by
Audubon's work. However, with Sir W. Jardine he published the
immensely popular and inexpensive 'Naturalist's Library'. These
pocket size books, with hand coloured engravings by various artists,
had for several years been given to Jemima as birthday presents by
her mother. The only man who stands on an equal footing with
Audubon is John Gould. This remarkable artist, scientist and
impresario was responsible for no less than eighteen folio works,
several in two volumes, comprising 2,999 different pictures, each
reproduced by lithography and hand-coloured. Gould was an
organiser *par excellence*, a designer, salesman and general manager;
but as an artist he was inferior to the majority of his team, which
included his wife Elizabeth, Edward Lear (whose superb *Illustrations*

Detail
18 × 25.3 cm. 'Redwing.' Inscribed
'length 8 inches, ½ wings 13.'
Birds from Nature (1862), pl. XII.
Birds from Nature (1868), pl. XII;
Birds from Moidart, p. 41.

of the Family of Psittacidae was the first book to treat a single family
of birds), Joseph Wolf, W. Hart and H. C. Richter.

Remarkable though these artists' work is, it is no more so than
Jemima's. She was a bird painter of very considerable skill and originality, and differed from them in that she painted her subjects from
life, or as she termed it 'from nature', and not from dead models as
Audubon did, or stuffed specimens as did Gould. She would go to
inordinate lengths to achieve a sketch, on occasions 'tubbing' across
deep ponds (a means of transport she employed well into middle age)
or hitching up her skirts and standing knee-deep in the water; or she
would climb high on the cliffs above Roshven to sit precariously beside
a buzzard's nest so as to draw the young. Owls were painted in their
nest high in a tree, from the rungs of a long ladder; nor did she let
the weather stop her, writing that on one occasion while attempting
to paint a swan the paint froze to her brush.

Her work was not purely illustrative. She adhered to the Pre-
Raphaelite principle of 'truth to nature' but added to this a firm belief
in scientific accuracy and precision. Many of her paintings have pen-
cilled notes, detailing the number of eggs, the material constitution
of the nest, or the measurements of the bird itself. She was recognised
as an ornithologist of some importance, and corresponded with many
of the most eminent naturalists of the period, notably Harting, Wolf,
and Darwin's cousin, Francis Galton.

In November 1859 Charles Darwin published *The Origin of Species*,
revising and correcting later editions usually to point out new evidence
for his theories. In the chapter on instinct, he refers to the ejection

of the young from a nest by a fledgling cuckoo, and in the 6th edition (1882) finds verification for his ideas from a 'trustworthy account' received by John Gould. This had its inception eleven years earlier on a hillside above Roshven. Gould, when writing about the cuckoo for his *Birds of Great Britain*, had suggested that it was the host parent bird, in tidying up the nest to make room for the young cuckoo, that accidentally caused the death of its own young. On publishing the text, he received from the Duke of Argyll a tracing from one of Jemima's drawings which clearly showed the young cuckoo itself ejecting pipit fledglings from their nest. Gould realised his mistake and had a lithograph and diagram made from the drawing, to be inserted as corrigenda. Jemima's attention had been drawn to the nest whilst out walking with friends, by seeing young pipit chicks struggling on a grassy slope. Thinking them accidentally fallen out, she replaced them in the nest. They were immediately ejected again. Cautiously she manoeuvred into a position from where she could see into the nest, which contained a young cuckoo 'perfectly naked, without the vestige of a feather, or even a hint of future feathers; its eyes were not yet opened and its neck seemed too weak to support the weight of its head . . . .' There follows a closely observed scientific account concluded in more emotional terms: 'The most singular thing of all was the direct purpose with which the blind little monster made for the open side of the nest, the only part where it could throw its burden down the bank. I think all the spectators felt the sort of horror and awe at the apparent inadequacy of the creature's intelligence to its acts that one might have felt at seeing a toothless hag raise a ghost by an incantation. It was horribly uncanny and gruesome!'

The resultant drawing, and Gould's publication of it, settled what had been one of the great ornithological arguments of the century. Edward Jenner, Montague and Muller, among others, had already recorded similar observations, but it was not until Jemima's drawing was published that visual evidence existed. Strangely it had first been published in 1871, not in a scientific journal but in a book called *The Pipits*, a companion volume to *Caw Caw* which was published that year. *The Pipits* is very similar in format, a story in verse, illustrated with black and white lithographs. When the book first appeared she was encouraged by 'several well-known naturalists' to publish an account of the details surrounding her observations. This she duly did in a letter published in *Nature* (14 March 1872) and *The Lancet* (2 July 1892), concluding that 'the sketch itself seems to me to be the only important addition I have made to the admirably accurate description given by Dr. Jenner . . .'.

Jemima's *Birds from Nature* (the punning title being a typical touch) was ready for publication in 1862 when some eleventh hour disaster occurred in which several of the plates were destroyed. For some weeks it looked as if the entire project might have to be scrapped, until eventually a decision was made to publish it in an attenuated form. Critically it was applauded, *The Scotsman* writing that 'We have seen no such birds since Bewick's. We say this not ignorant of the magnificent plates by Selby, Audubon, Wilson and Gould.' Ruskin

Detail
13 × 13.6 cm. Ink and wash drawing. Young cuckoo ejecting Meadow Pipit fledglings from the nest. This version re-drawn from the original.

Detail
16.5 × 21 cm. Watercolour. August 1867.
Harvesting in the 'bank field', Roshven.
Jemima drawing the scene from
horseback.

however, in a letter to Lady Trevelyan dated 26 December 1861, commented: 'A book of birds had just come in from Mrs Blackburn. What a singular or rather Pre-Raphaelite gift this talented Lady has in uglifying everything. The staring likeness of a Bird may be made as disagreeable as the staring likeness of any human being.'

Jemima was not happy with the book, and began to rework the damaged plates with the intention that it should be republished. Six years passed before it duly reappeared, with an additional twenty two plates which Jemima insisted be sent to subscribers to the original version free of charge. She can only have been delighted with it in its republished form, for it is a beautiful book. Seven copies were hand-coloured, six for sale to the general public, the last a birthday present to a special friend. It is unfortunate that further coloured copies were not produced, as one cannot help but feel that the decline in her reputation since her death is at least partly due to this. Understandably it was well received both by the critics and the general public—*The Athenaeum* reckoning that 'these are amongst the most perfect and conscientiously executed works we have ever met with'. *The Scotsman*'s critic was no less fulsome in his praise: 'When some portion of this splendid and interesting volume was published two or three years ago, we felt the difficulty of conveying by any words of praise or description an adequate idea of its impressive yet unobtrusive beauty.' He commented perceptively that the illustrations were 'not merely of the shapes and proportions of the birds but . . . above all represent not the species merely, but the individual—not a bird but the bird . . . . Mrs. Blackburn gives us distinct, spirited and faithful portraits of each bird that has sat to her. She is especially successful where success might seem most difficult in giving expression to the eyes and bills . . . look at those infant black guillemots . . . . one is as clearly expressive of calm resolution and sober dignity as the other is [of] querulousness and fidgityness; you can safely predict for one long life, fat, prosperity, for the other a brief and troubled career . . . .'

Joseph Wolf wrote her a long congratulatory letter praising her conscientious and truthful work . . . 'The heads and expressions of your Birds are particularly good and true and what I have always liked in your drawings of horses and other animals, the legs and feet, are here also good, which can only be the result of close and careful study. With regards to your backgrounds of foliage, and I must say it is not easy to make such careful work suitable as a background, but you have succeeded well by giving graceful stalks and leaves in outline and by putting in a touch of depth only where required. In avoiding hard outlines of single feathers and over precision of their markings you have preserved an agreeable breadth and have produced pictures of birds as birds are generally seen. The reverse of this subordination of detail forms a great fault in Gould's drawings; his pastel plumage without light shade or perspective in the markings spoils the form by flattening it and instead of showing the round body of a bird it often looks more like a mere map of its markings. Besides as Mr Gould has never drawn birds direct from the life his figures must be more or less conventional and consequently there are very few of them so characteristick [*sic*] as those of yours which are done direct from the life and it is only the deplorable state of general ignorance in the matter even among naturalists which stands in the way of making this apparent at a glance. In birds most people look for the colours, few see the actual form, and this leads me to think that for a longer sale of your book coloured copies would perhaps be more suitable than plain ones.

'I shall of course avail myself of every opportunity to recommend your "Birds" as I have here said they deserve and I trust that their own merits will ultimately make them as popular.'

One of the problems that surrounded the 1862 version of *Birds from Nature* was that the accident to the lithographic plates occurred when Jemima was out of the country. The previous year her brother George, who had suffered from tuberculosis for many years, had been advised to spend the winter in a warmer climate. He had become an irascible and difficult man, and firmly refused to undertake a journey to Egypt unless he was accompanied by his sister. She was, as we have seen, extremely busy, and was reluctant to leave her family. However, it was obvious that he was seriously ill and so, after long discussions with Hugh, she agreed to go. Egypt had long fascinated her; her brother Andrew's descriptions of the country, and his insistence that she should visit it some day, heightened her curiosity. It was decided that the party should consist of George and Jemima, their nephew Colin Mackenzie, a young man who was very friendly with George and who could act as his companion, and, as it was discovered that he could travel free, the eleven-year-old William. All the organising was left to Colin and Jemima, although by the meticulous way this was approached one suspects Hugh of lending a hand. They wrote to various authorities who they knew had travelled in the country, asking for advice, including Charles Wilson of the Glasgow School of Design on the question of what drawing and painting materials to take.

Eventually all was prepared and the party departed for Liverpool by train, from where on 10 October they set sail aboard the *Palestine*. The first few days proved to be exceptionally stormy and Colin recorded in his journal '. . . Mrs Hugh up on deck and looking better. I begin to regain consciousness and find myself domiciled in a swamp of tea toast and chicken bones, so conclude that attempts have been made to feed me.' The weather continued to be uncomfortably rough all the way to Malta, but even so, they decided that instead of unpacking and transferring ships, they would stay aboard the *Palestine* and visit Smyrna and Constantinople before disembarking at Malta on the return journey.

The few letters that survive from this period give a glimpse of the close relationships that existed within the Blackburn family. They delighted in giving each other nicknames, Professor Hugh being known variously as Drodson or Faller, Jemima as Bim or Muller, William as Bill or Massei, Margaret as Peggy, Womany or Lady. Hugh never seems to have had a nickname although when small was known as Love; Colin Mackenzie was referred to as Coonie or κυνη. Jemima's letters slip back and forth between the first and third persons with endearing ease. From Constantinople on the first of November she wrote:

Dear Hugh,

Here is Muller sitting in the harbour of Constantinople of all places in the world only think of sailing up the Dardanelles that we used to learn in Geography books and queer places they are—quite narrow with strange castles on each side—show it to Womany on the map . . . . I am doing lots of sketches of people; a lot came on board from Syra and more from Galipoli and when they perceived I was drawing them more and more came and sat for their pictures, they came all about the saloon windows looking in so I drew them from the inside . . . you have no notion how queer it all is . . . . The approach to Constantinople was very beautiful, but just after that a dense fog came on which obscured everything and prevented our getting into the harbour.—Mosques are strange and pretty I think—but the streets and bazaars and above all the women are the queerest things you ever saw—very short in height about up to my chin and in circumference equal to Barbara McFee—but I guess you will see lots of them in my sketches . . . . I wonder very much what you are all after, whether Womany has got her governess—and dear Love—I look at his photograph often—I will write often to let you know where and how we are but the description part is best done in the sketches. Foreign climate is as yet a—humbug, I wonder if Egypt is a humbug too—but it is great fun I wish old Drodson could see it, in haste

Muller

My Dear Faller,

Constantinople is the rummest place I ever saw but I have seen cleaner and all the stinks of the vennel and other places are nothing to the smell at the landing place and we have got a guide called Moses and and [sic] we went into a shop and if you had seen Muller with her cigar threatening Moses if you dont make a good bargain puff you will never have any employment in the Palestine again puff puff. At the top of a hill I caught two such wonderful insects one was called a walking leaf the other was a wonderful thing with an enormous tail. bye the bye the pricly [sic] pears are all rot the apples and pears are nothing great plenty oranges quines [sic] and lemons. the melons and especially the water melons are delightful things the rahathacoum is very good and we will send you some

Yours
Mr William Blackburn esq.

Pet Husband,

Here she is really enjoying herself at last after all—at Smyrna it is a strange place as completely Eastern as possible much nicer than Constantinople [though] that was good too, but the dunes here are queerer still and being among strings of camels loaded with figs it is much to her fancy . . . . She would very much like to have him here—wonders how he would like it—Massey is so happy enjoying life first rate—I think he will not forget it . . . we are anchored out in the bay half a mile or so from shore— the view [is] beautiful and the sunsets and moonlights first rate— the pinkness of the hills and pale green of the sky making—but so effervescent I have not got a grip of it yet—I suppose we shall have the like in Egypt. We took a ride on cuddies today which Massey much enjoyed—one is getting so used to the manners and customs of Turks and Easterners that I expect we shall feel quite at home when we get to Egypt . . .   . . . The Fieldins started an idea of taking [in] Rome on the way home in Spring, which George took up a good deal. I would like it well enough if old Drodson would come and do it too. It would be dull for him to come there all alone but he might think of it, it would then be "work done . . ." she can manage with camels and shop in bazaars herself but the pictures etc would not be $\frac{1}{2}$ without him. She was a long time in getting over leaving her husband but in this place she is so absorbed as gone out of her self with the strangeness that she can think of nothing else, till she shuts her eyes in her wee lonely beddie with her son over head and her pet starling hanging up—and then she wished she could nestle in his beardie—you see the spirit of travel as B Jim would call it is upon her and she is going to make the best of it all—every time she thinks of him she rushes to her drawing to do some more for him . . . .'

This letter is, sadly, incomplete. On reaching Malta they found letters from the Professor and Margaret awaiting them, telling of the accident which had upset the publication of *Birds from Nature*.

   . . . I wish the book had gone right it is such a bother after telling so many people about it—its coming to nothing—but she is too far away to give any advise [*sic*] about it, she must just not think about it but go ahead with her foreign sketches, she is making a very fine one of the sultan at Constant- . . . . Dr Horne called today, he used to know Peter and Colin in Edinburgh long ago and did experiments with laughing gas with Colin and thinks that one of their experiments must have been performed on you . . . . Do you think I should send home my drawings from here which I finish for fear of anything coming over them. If I do I will ensure [*sic*] them write me what you think

in haste
Bim

Detail
28 × 22 cm. Watercolour and body
colour. 1 November 1861. A Procession
in Constantinople.

My Dear Faller,

read unto Lady, Sir, and Babby I hough this I went with Mrs Forde, G.W and Muller to see a review but we were too late and met them marching home . . . . By the way Muller has not grown fat yet but she says she intends to in the Nile boat for she has not time here.

After a wait of some three weeks in Malta they were able to board the P. & O. ship *Elora*, bound for Alexandria, and on arrival begin their expeditions up the Nile.

The journey was slow and leisurely, and it was the end of February before they reached Wadi Halfa. To progress from here up to the second cataract at Abu Seir either a further small boat had to be hired or a journey made across the desert. Colin reports in his journal that the owners of the boat 'asked for £1—and would not be beaten down. We decided that Mrs Hugh and Bill should ride off . . . and see what matters were like—and accordingly by 8 o'clock they had got their breakfast and started; they returned about 2 o'clock reporting the view from Abooseer to be strange, like a number of carts of coal coupit into the river—eerie, but not pretty—the ride long and rather heavy . . .' The following morning Colin and William trekked to the cataract, and on their return the boat was turned round and 'the rowers broke out in their song and hurrah for home and letters again'. On reaching midstream the rowers stopped and the boat drifted down in the current until the sun began to sink into the west; then rowing to the bank they halted and played cards in the warm desert evening, retiring to bed only when the Southern Cross hung low in the sky.

On the day that the Blackburn/Wedderburn party had turned north of Abu Seir a party comprising H.R.H. The Prince of Wales, General Bruce, Major Tweesdale, Captain Keppel, the Hon R. Meade, Dr Minton, Captain Power, Dean Stanley and Consul-General Colquhoun had left Cairo, and sailed south up the Nile. This tour to the Holy Lands had been arranged before Prince Albert's death on 13 December 1861 and only after much discussion had it been decided that it should go ahead. Inevitably the two parties' paths had to cross.

Rumours that the Prince of Wales was in Egypt and bound up the Nile had reached Jemima and the others, but only on the morning of 12 March had it been confirmed: 'the smoke of a steamer was seen far away to the north about 2 o'clock; we were all excitement. By 2.30 the "cortege" passed us. First came a Government steamer with the crescent and star flying to clear the way, next came Fadeh Basha's private yacht with himself in solitary state [in] an armchair on the stern deck, with the crescent and star again, towing up Mr Colquhoun in a Dahabieh with a Union Jack which we saluted, next came Said Basha's own steam yacht towing a large Dahabieh on the poop deck of which the Prince was seated and opposite him the Basha with their respective attendants; the Prince rose and took off his wideawake to us—so of course we off with our bonnets, and popped off the revolver for the Prince and the double barrel for the Basha—they swiftly disappeared up the river—such was our glimpse of "El Elbr el Soultan

Ingéleez". Of said Basha, whom, to say the truth, I was more anxious to see of the two, I could see nothing, but a fattish coarse looking back in an armchair.'

Two days later the Prince's party overtook them on the way back north. The two boats shared a mooring, enabling Mr Colquhoun to hand to Jemima two telegrams containing disturbing news, one to say that the Professor Hugh was seriously ill with typhoid, the other to say he was recovering. Understandably, she became anxious to reach Thebes where they had hopes of being able to pick up mail. Colin, who had spent a good deal of his time learning Egyptian (to Jemima's disgust, she thinking his time better spent in sightseeing), explained this to the crew, and very soon (after financial inducement) 'the kind hearted fellows were enlisted to the cause'. As darkness fell the boat hit a sand bank but 'the crew to a man took to the water and hove us off'. They reached Luxor the following evening and were relieved to read in the letters which were indeed awaiting them, that Hugh was well on the road to recovery. There was a great deal of anxiety within the ranks of the crew as to what the news was and, wrote Colin, 'Achmet Ali's sentiment I think too was honest—after I had paid him over the money I promised as backsheish, I said, "Well, Achmet my father"—(a constant form of address to the older sailors in my mouth)—"are you satisfied—is the backsheish paid in full toll?" He answered, "God increase your prosperity my master, you are good and the lady is good indeed but the backsheish is of no moment—I took one look at the Lady's face and at once I rowed my oar like a huge efreet." '

The news being favourable, and in view of the effort expended by the crew, it was decided that they would halt for three days at Thebes, whose ruins were considered the most stupendous of their kind in the world. Jemima was keen to sketch the famous temples at Karnak, and set out early next day, a Sunday. Unbeknown to her the Prince had suggested to Canon Stanley that a service be held in the great hall of Karnak. 'Mrs Hugh . . . was found and introduced', recorded Colin, 'also Mr William for whom H R H made up a cigarette. G.W. and I rode there later in the day, saw Dr Minto & Col Bruce—2 nice bodies—Canon Stanley . . . a perky jerky dried up body, & H R H, a decent unaffected cheery body. G.W. was introduced. Mrs Hugh & Bill took a bit of luncheon—we didn't . . . .' Francis Bedford (who had been commissioned to act as official photographer to the Prince's party) took a fine picture of the group after lunch, the Prince helping to pose the gathering, though the result did not please Jemima.

Over the following two days Jemima and William were invited to join the Prince of Wales on his exploration of the Karnak temples. The Prince became very friendly with William, and on the evening before their departure invited him to dinner.

In the morning it was discovered, to the crew's great joy, that Mr Colquhoun had arranged with General Bruce for their boat to be towed with the Prince's party as far as Cairo, from where William and Jemima travelled as quickly as possible to Alexandria and caught the first ship for Britain.

The *Euphrosyne* seems to have been a particularly uncomfortable vessel, and they had a rather unpleasant crossing to Malta. On their arrival they realised that it would be quicker, and probably more comfortable, to cross to Marseilles and complete the journey overland. This they duly did, reaching Glasgow to find Hugh very much recovered. A few days after their return George Mackenzie, Colin's brother, was at work in a solicitor's office in Edinburgh when he was handed a note: '*Euphrosyne*—lost at Corrobedo near Lisbon—crew saved—total wreck'. His colleague had added in pencil, 'Is this not the ship your brother's friend Mrs. Blackburn was coming home in? I know of no further particulars but suppose the passengers are saved too.' It cannot have taken him too long to ascertain the true position. However in Malta, where George and Colin had now arrived, the news caused much consternation, and it took several letters before they understood that Jemima and William were, so to speak, home and dry. Most of their luggage seems to have gone down with the ship, but fortunately either Jemima carried her drawing portfolio with her, or, as she had suggested, sent the paintings home as she completed them.

The remainder of the summer was spent quietly at Roshven. The rebuilding of the house had been completed some three years earlier, and the work on the extensive landscaping of the grounds was progressing well, work that within twenty years would prompt Father MacDonald to write that it had been 'conducted with much taste and judgement . . . [and had] made Roshven [into] one of the loveliest places in the Western Highlands'. Hugh spent much of his period of convalescence studying and listing the flora of the immediate area. He belonged to, possibly, the last generation that did not see the arts and science as mutually exclusive; rather science provided a firmer foundation for aesthetic response. Scientific methods of the time involved walking, collecting, observing, drawing and listing, occupations ideally suited to his (and Jemima's) temperament, the eventual purpose being identical to that of the theologian, namely to reveal the glory of God in His divine ordering of the Universe. Science was changing, a fact of which Hugh was well aware. However he, like Clerk-Maxwell, had no difficulty in assimilating these contemporary discoveries to his faith.

GLASGOW CATHEDRAL sat at the top of the city's High Street, presiding over what remained of medieval Glasgow. It had been built from 1136 and was, according to Scott in *Rob Roy*, 'a braw kirk [with] nane o' your whigmaleeries and curliewurlies, and open-steek hems about it—a solid, well-jointed mason-wark, that will stand as lang as the warld, keep hands and gun powther aff it'. It had been heavily restored between 1835 and 1856, during which period a proposal was made to fill its windows with stained glass. This was taken up with great enthusiasm by a large and influential body of subscribers, and by 1859 the first window was installed. Most of the work was carried out by the fashionable Königliche Glasmalereianstalt

Munich, partly on the advice of Charles Winston, the leading stained glass expert of his day. A few of the windows were made in Edinburgh and London, and Jemima designed one of these as a memorial to her father. It is a typical flowing and rounded composition, somewhat pre-Raphaelite in style, and must have looked quite *avant garde* when seen amongst the dark, richly coloured, and monotonously designed Munich windows.

Glasgow's polluted atmosphere caused many of the German windows to fade prematurely, and by the 1930's most were in extremely poor condition. In an inspired move initiated by the minister of the time, the Rev. Dr A. Nevile Davidson, it was decided to remove the Munich glass and replace it with windows designed by contemporary artists. The scheme, carried out with much taste and judgement, enhances one of the most beautiful buildings in Northern Europe. Jemima's window, in the Blackadder Aisle, was left in place and fits in well with its more modern neighbours, seeming with hindsight to have as much to do with Art Nouveau as Pre-Raphaelitism.

She designed two other windows, both as memorials to members of the Robertson family, friends and neighbours at Roshven. These, in the south wall of the tiny Kinlochmoidart Chapel, also have a strikingly contemporary feel, and contrive to make the other windows of similar, or later, date appear conservative and uninspired.

The magazine *Good Words* was a popular family publication with a circulation amongst 70,000 readers. Its editor, the Rev. Norman Macleod, was a frequent visitor to the Blackburns in Glasgow, and in 1861 had suggested that the magazine should serialise 'Illustrations from Scripture'. The result helped greatly to popularise her work, and prompted the young George du Maurier, in a letter to his mother, to write, 'The tracing of my Aunt's sketch was most delightful, she is a foolish little lady not to cultivate so great a gift of God, which properly trained would make her plenty of money and a stunning name, look at Mrs Blackburn who has monopolised the large page of *Good Words* and is decidedly well paid for it too, and courted more for her talent than ever she could be for the title she possesses in common with some 2,500 other ladies.' While his assertion that she monopolised *Good Words* is certainly an exaggeration, over the next ten years she did become a frequent and popular contributor.

Determining the income she derived from her illustrative work is not easy. She had declined royalties from the publication of 'Illustrations from Scripture', requesting instead that she be given some free copies to distribute among friends. Despite this, by the mid-1860s she was, as Du Maurier says, 'decidedly well paid', and able to turn her private income to projects within her own area of concern. She had been appalled to discover that the shopkeepers in Moidart made up for the 'fewness of the dealings by the enormity of the profits', and accordingly purchased the best groceries she could find in Glasgow at wholesale prices and then, on one day a week, sold them to people on the estate at no profit. This proved to be so successful that before long 'the shop' stocked dry goods, cloths, and clothing, all of which were supplied on the same favourable terms. When in

1881 a severe hurricane, accompanied by an extraordinary high tide, destroyed nearly every boat in Loch Ailort—an event of potentially tragic proportions as many of the families relied upon fishing for their livelihood—'she was able to present new boats to all who had lost their own along a twenty mile stretch of coastline out of the earnings of her pencil . . . not requiring any aid even from her husband'.

On 17 March 1865, two months before her forty second birthday, she gave birth to a third son, Alan, an event which may have given rise to the story of an unnamed Professor at Glasgow University whose wife it was known had just had a baby. The Professor on entering his classroom the next morning was loudly cheered. 'Silence, gentlemen', he called, 'these accidents will happen in the best regulated families'.

Before the family could leave Glasgow for Roshven at the end of term, news came from Edinburgh that George Wedderburn, whose health had declined steadily since returning from Egypt, had died on the first of May. He was buried in the city's Dean Cemetery, and although there is no direct evidence, it can be presumed that Hugh, at least, attended the funeral.

During the summer the family quickly fitted into the routine of life at Roshven. William, by now a handsome and healthy lad of fifteen, organised his brother and sister—and sometimes even father—to go into the hills in search of geological specimens, or to go birdnesting or fishing on the loch. Margaret joined in these expeditions with varying degrees of enthusiasm. She had her mother's love of ornithology, and was particularly good at finding birds' nests. She took an interest in photography and with her father began to devise methods of photographing birds in the wild. In later years she became friendly with the great exponents of bird photography, Richard and Cherry Kearton, but there is little evidence that they had any particular influence on what remained for her principally a hobby. It seems that Jemima planned a volume of *Animals from Nature* as a companion to the *Birds*, and during the summer she, William, and Margaret went on a sailing trip to the Hyskeir Islands to study seals; but despite several similar trips it was a project that for one reason or another was never realised.

An exhibition of watercolours held by McLure and Sons in their Buchanan Street gallery in 1866, gives an example of Jemima's astute commercial judgement. Barely a month after the republication of *Birds from Nature* she exhibited two 'ornithological studies'. The extent of her renown at this point can be gauged by a letter which arrived from Canada in March, addressed simply to 'Mrs Hugh Blackburn, author of *Birds from Nature*, (in or near) Glasgow, Scotland', a letter which, incidentally, was delivered in a little under two weeks.

These were years of great contentment for the Blackburns. The surroundings of the new university buildings were pleasant, and no longer was the winter in Glasgow something that had to be endured. Jemima worked on illustrations to a book by the noted English historian J. A. Froud, *The Cats Pilgrimage*. This obviously is not an academic treatise. It relates the adventures of a cat as it tries to deter-

Detail
21.3 × 18.5 cm. Ink and watercolour.
7 September 1871. Left to right:
Sir William Thomson, Hugh, James
Thomson, and Prof. Helmholtz discussing the flight of birds at Roshven.

mine the true meaning of life. Both story and illustrations are quaint and full of a gentle humour: it is arguably the finest of her fairy tale or fable books.

Professor Hugh and William Thomson were engaged in the production of a new edition of Newton's seminal *Principia Mathematica*, and Thomson was a frequent visitor both in Glasgow and at Roshven. In September 1871 he arrived in his yacht *Lalla Rookh* with a party that included his brother, the noted engineer James, and the distinguished German physicist Professor Helmholtz, who was involved in work on wave theory with Thomson. Helmholtz wrote from Roshven on 9 September: 'W.T. was very eager to arrive here, where his colleague Mr Blackburn . . . has a lonely property, a very lovely spot on a bay between the loveliest of mountains. The Atlantic showed itself this time very friendly and we came quickly here, so that in the afternoon we could take an excursion with the family and dined with them . . . Mrs B has a remarkable talent for painting animals. She fashions all her doings and household ways to suit her professional tastes . . . it was all very friendly and unconstrained. W.T. presumed so far on the freedom of his surroundings that he always carried his mathematical note book about with him, and would begin to calculate in the midst of company if anything occurred to him, which was treated with certain awe by the party. How would it be if I accustomed the Berliners to the same proceedings?'

James Thomson, in a letter to his wife a day earlier, wrote 'we . . . anchored in shallow water in front of Roshven House. We went ashore and saw Prof and Mrs B and their 3 sons and 1 daughter also Mr Ferguson . . . also John Thomson. We all went to Goat Island; and climbed to the top. It is very steep. On top there is a great vitrified fort of quite prehistoric times . . . . We arranged last night that if today were fine enough the Blackburns and their party would come out to the *L.R.* and we would all sail in the yacht to Eigg . . . . The day is wet and very windy: and I suppose we shall stay partly in the yacht and partly on shore with the Blackburns . . . . We saw some admirable drawings yesterday evening done by Mrs Blackburn. One was a drawing of a baby cuckoo shoving the other young birds older than itself out of the nest. She sketched it while the process was going on.'

It must have been on this occasion that the story is told of William Thomson, Hugh, and sundry other academics being becalmed whilst in the Sound of Arisaig. Whilst the women indulged in light-hearted conversation the menfolk amused themselves by calculating the equations of motion of the waves lapping the side of the boat.

The Blackburns were renowned for their hospitality. At Roshven the dining room was one of the finest rooms in the house. Situated on the first floor, it commanded magnificent views out over the bay to the Ardnish and Arisaig peninsulas and further to the mountains of Rhum and Skye. The room was panelled in wood with an unusual Egyptian-style painted plaster cornice. Large paintings of groups of birds, by Jemima, were set into the walls, and a fire burned brightly in the solid stone fireplace. On a wild winter's night, with the long thick curtains drawn against the crashing of the sea and howling wind, it was a room of warm serenity; in summer, when a fire was lit purely for show and the long warm evening light flooded through the windows, one of quiet but spectacular beauty. At the dinner table could be found sitting 'the Radical and the Conservative, the Dissenter and the Churchman, the Roman Catholic and the Protestant'. Their taste as hosts was thoroughly catholic.

After dinner entertainment varied considerably, from serious and earnest discussions on science and art, to musical recitals and gambling. One such session is described by a neighbour; there were 'two whist tables, one highly scientific consisting of Mr and Mrs Robertson, Mr Alan Blackburn and F; the other desperately serious, Mr Hope (an academic), Mr Hunter, J. and Mr William Blackburn.' On other evenings 'dancing is begun and goes on with increasing vigour' until three in the morning.

Politics was of course a constant subject for dinner and after-dinner conversation. After all, these were exciting times, a fact realised to the full in Scotland, where the public eagerly followed the exchanges in the personal duel between Gladstone and Disraeli. Curiously Gladstone, an English High Churchman, was well respected, indeed revered, in many Scots homes; but not however at Roshven. Although Hugh appears to have been virtually apolitical, Jemima made up for it by being a fervent admirer of Disraeli. If a guest 'were a disciple of the Radical school' he would require to defend his convictions with a keen and skilled debater. On one occasion when the daughters of a neighbour were staying at Roshven they recorded that 'F had innocently remarked that she was a Radical and found the whole party against her. Mrs Blackburn refused for a long time to believe her ears . . . and F had only the consciousness of a good cause to support her.' With such strength of feeling it can be imagined how much Jemima enjoyed entertaining Disraeli when, in November 1873, he came to Glasgow to make a speech after his election to the post of Rector of the University.

The following February, Hugh and Jemima set out on a three-month tour of Italy, a trip which had been planned and talked about ever since Jemima had sown its seeds in a letter from the Gulf of Smyrna nearly eleven years before. They travelled from Turin to Rome, Naples and Sorrento, Amalfi and Pisa before eventually ending up in Florence. Jemima, as in their previous visit, worked prodigiously, producing one hundred and sixty two paintings; and when time would not permit a sketch to be made she would attempt to buy a photograph of the subject.

Some months before his death Hugh's friend and colleague, Professor J. M. Rankine (a man whose engineering genius had masterminded the piping of drinking water to Glasgow from Loch Katrine and thus helped to eradicate cholera from the city) brought Jemima a small note book in which he had written several fables which he wished her to illustrate. He had been a close family friend for many years, and she had no hesitation in agreeing to his request, eventually, in 1874, publishing a small book entitled *Songs and Fables*. The illustrations are perhaps not of the same quality as her earlier work but they show great imagination, some being almost surrealistic in content, and typically idiosyncratic.

For many years the Blackburns had been trying to persuade Ruskin to visit Roshven, an invitation he never took up although the possibility was obviously on his mind, for in his diary on 27 July 1874 he noted: 'Slept well, after careful and troublesome thought about Brantswood, and dreamed with absurd rationality about Mrs Blackburn inviting me to come and visit Scotland, and I replying politely that I had better know it than see it, and could perfectly know it by her description.' Four years later his mind sadly began to slip; and although his friends in mistaken kindness, reinstated him as Slade Professor at Oxford, his infirmity became increasingly evident. A month before he left Oxford for good he wrote the following enigmatic entry in his diary: 'Feb. 22 1885 Sunday. Woke at one in the morning with bad heartburn. Made various good resolutions about more exercise and less port, and slept ever since and find a lot of lovely things— above all the hawk's feather—waiting me at bottom of stairs fresh from Herne Hill. D.G. Hawk's feather sets me thinking of Mrs. Blackburns d - - - d impudence, and I lose ten minutes and a lot of temper in ideally smashing her.'

Elizabeth Rigby, Lady Eastlake, was an influential voice within the Victorian world. As a young woman she had been a great enthusiast for photography, and appears in many of the calotypes of Hill and Adamson. She married Sir Charles Lock Eastlake, an historical painter who became President of the Royal Academy and director of the National Gallery. After his death in 1865 she became an influential writer on aesthetic matters. It is difficult to say just where and when she and Jemima became acquainted. On 16 June 1876 she wrote:

Dear Mrs Blackburn,
The sight of your drawings just before I left London so filled my mind with thoughts of them that I longed and even intended writing you a few lines. But I was too busy and every day that passed made me feel less bold to do it. Now I have had dear Isabella . . . with me for a week, and we have talked so much of those matchless drawings that my boldness has returned! I must tell you therefore if I can the exceeding admiration with which they inspired me something akin to that speechless kind with which I have stood before an old master. I have tried to define in my mind what it is that so delights one. I think it is the exceeding purity of feeling both in colour and taste . . . [and] absence of all convention, manner and chigne [?]. I instructed to you a great study of Turner, but I have since felt the simple truth of your words, that you had studied *Nature*. In that respect however is your likeness to certain prime qualities in Turner, for you have both looked at the same thing in the same way.
I hear of your industry—I cannot wonder at it! Art is the happiest of all attainments, its practice is so tranquillising to the artist—so unencroaching on the liking of others . . . .
Believe me dear Mrs Blackburn
yrs truly   Eliz. Eastlake

Detail
10.75 × 15 cm. Watercolour. 18 October 1876. The dustman and milkman in Valencia.

The drawings to which Elizabeth Eastlake refers are probably Jemima's exhibits in an exhibition held in the Dudley Gallery during 1875.

In October and November of 1876 Hugh and Jemima travelled in Spain, once more the stimulus of a foreign country prompting Jemima to produce an enormous quantity of work—one hundred and thirty paintings, again augmented by photographs. It is strange, therefore, to find that over the following year she appears to have painted next to nothing. There is no ready explanation for this, unless she were ill in some way. But happily new scenes were to revive her creativity.

John Burns was the son of the co-founder of the Cunard shipping line, and he had been a friend of the Blackburns for many years. During the early part of 1878 a letter from him was delivered to Jemima in Glasgow, inviting her on a cruise to Iceland and the Arctic. Her son Alan was unwell at the time and she was undecided as to what her answer should be. He speedily persuaded his mother that she would be foolish to refuse.

The party, when assembled at Wemyss Bay, numbered five ladies and eleven gentlemen, and included in their ranks the novelist Anthony Trollope. They embarked in the *Mastiff* on Saturday 22 June, setting sail for St Kilda, a group of islands then undergoing something of a tourist boom. Unfortunately they arrived in mist and rain, and could not appreciate the awe-inspiring scenery of the islands, scenery which would prompt a visitor the following year to write 'had we not heard of it before, we should have said that if inhabited it must be by monsters'. The islanders were far from monstrous, although when Jemima attempted to sketch some of the women with their children, they turned away, one woman hiding her child. Jemima, thinking they must have some superstitious reason, made a 'mental photograph' and completed her sketch from memory. She was astounded to learn later that the islanders, showing a sound capitalist philosophy, were so bothered by tourists taking their like-

21.4 × 25.6 cm. Watercolour.
Investigating an eagle's nest above
Loch Ailort. Left to right: Jemima,
Vere Saville, 'Gracie', Sybil Kirkland,
Mrs Kirkland, Margaret.

nesses in one way or another that they charged five shillings for the sitting. 'The Mastiffs', as the party called themselves, stayed only a few hours before circumnavigating the archipelago and sailing for Torshavn in the Faroes—a town which, on their arrival, Jemima found to be one of the prettiest she had seen, proceeding despite the lateness of the hour (11.30 pm) to execute some pencil sketches.

It had been their intention to sail into the Arctic Circle to see the midnight sun but, due to poor weather and reports of unseasonal ice off the north coast of Iceland, they changed their plans and sailed for Reykjavik. This in itself was not without its problems. They were at first unable to leave Torshavn because of rough seas and, even when eventually getting under way, found it 'less rough than we expected but still pretty bad'. Jemima had to sit on the cabin floor with her legs braced against the berths to be steady enough to enable her to complete a drawing.

Seventy miles inland from Reykjavik are the great geysers, a phenomenon described in graphic detail by nearly all the early travellers in Iceland. They were plainly something that had to be seen. The expedition that was mounted called for considerable organisation. Sixty five ponies were engaged to carry a hundredweight of cooked meat, crockery, cooking utensils, tents, blankets, mattresses for the ladies, and the carpetbags of the party. Obviously no undue hardship was to be endured in a four-day trip. Jemima, a seasoned traveller, preferred to travel light, carrying everything she needed, but for a Shetland shawl and a cloak, on her own pony in a pair of coarse woollen saddlebags she had bought the previous year in Barcelona. The start of the expedition was little short of pure farce. 'The Mastiffs, all in high spirits and desirous of displaying their horsemanship, scampered off as hard as they could go. During the first mile the road was strewed with loose packages and dropped cloaks and handkerchiefs, one gentleman galloped for some way with his valise hanging to the pony's tail . . . and some ladies' saddles came round, all but spilling the riders.'

The following day, still in high good humour, the party reached the geysers and waited for many hours in the vain hope of seeing an eruption. Jemima made a series of drawings which indicate this frustration and the high spirits with which the 'Mastiffs' combatted it. In the first, the party peers into a crater—this is entitled 'Inspection'; the following one, labelled 'Incantation', shows them holding hands and dancing around it; the third, 'Expectation', has them peering once again into the depths of the crater, to be rewarded with 'Eruption', the fourth of the sequence. Eventually, without having witnessed more than a minor eruption, they began the return journey.

The ladies received permission to sleep in the church at Thingvalla, and at first light Jemima 'escaped quietly by climbing over the pews.' Outside she met a fellow 'Mastiff' and, both being interested in natural history, they decided to take a boat and watch the birds on a neighbouring island. After some hours pleasantly spent, hunger compelled them to return for breakfast, 'though we had to wait some time for it, as our companions, who had been sleeping the sleep of the

just all morning, were only beginning to arouse themselves about mid-day'. The journey back to Reykjavik was accomplished at a leisurely pace. After a bathe in the sea or the tub, according to taste, and break-fast on board the *Mastiff*, they went on shore to take leave of their hosts. They sailed at midday with the thought that whereas travellers in other countries are tempted to quote 'Where every prospect pleases, and man alone is vile', the Icelander is superior to his country.

On their return to Britain Anthony Trollope and Jemima col-laborated in an account of the trip, *How the Mastiffs went to Iceland*, published privately in 1878. It is a typically idiosyncratic account both by author and illustrator. Trollope described Jemima as 'unlike anyone else he had known', and certainly they must have been a formi-dable pair, as both delighted in debate and argument and both showed extraordinary industry within their own fields. Trollope regularly completed forty pages of two hundred and fifty words a week; Jemima on this trip produced fifty six paintings and drawings in fifteen days. They played chess together and shared a passion for riding and hunt-ing, which Trollope had been forced to give up the previous March: she would have understood just how heart-breaking he had found the disposal of his horses. In her memoirs she refers to him as 'Tony'

16.6 × 20.2 cm. Watercolour over pencil. 'Expectation.' Anthony Trollope standing to left of centre, wearing a dark hat. Iceland 1878.

Trollope. The only other people on record to do this are his mother, when he was a small boy, and an old friend, George Augustus Sala, who penned an accurate word portrait of the man on the title page of his copy of Trollope's autobiography: 'Crusty, quarrelsome, wrongheaded, prejudiced, obstinate, kind hearted and thoroughly honest old Tony Trollope'.

Jemima published her own account of the expedition in *Good Words*. Strangely she makes no mention of Trollope, and in all but one of her illustrations to accompany the article his figure is omitted, even though it appears in the originals. Some years earlier the editor of *Good Words*, Norman Macleod, had commissioned a novel from Trollope which he had then refused to use, writing in explanation a rather patronising letter. It would have been characteristic if Trollope had insisted to Jemima that he did not wish to appear between the covers of the magazine in any form whatsoever.

The years of quiet content came to an end, and 1879 proved sad and worrying. On 4 January, Jemima's brother John died at his home in London. He had had a distinguished career, rising to the rank of Major-General in the Bengal Staff Corps, and had been awarded a medal and two clasps at the battle of Gujerat.

Throughout the decade Hugh had encountered increasing problems with his hearing, and by 1879 it was so impaired that he resigned his post at the University. Inevitably he became an increasingly solitary figure. He could no longer enjoy music, his prime source of relaxation, and so threw his energies into further improving Roshven, and into a detailed study of the Blackburn genealogy. He continued his study of the flora of the area, and seems to have contemplated publishing a paper on naked-eyed medusae for which he had been making copious notes for many years.

While her husband's deafness was obviously a source of worry to Jemima, she was also concerned about young Hugh, who had joined The Buffs (the third regiment of the line, later the East Kent) and had been posted to South Africa to fight in what became known as the Zulu War.

The final blow in this traumatic year came in November with the news of Clerk-Maxwell's death at Glenlair. He had been ill for some months, probably with cancer of the stomach; and although he had tried to work on, he had been told by Dr Sanders of Edinburgh on 2 October that he had not more than a month to live. He accepted this with calm resignation. As Dr Paget recalled, 'He wished to live until the expected arrival from Edinburgh of his friend and relative Mr Colin Mackenzie . . . [and when it came] no man ever met death more consciously or more calmly.' Colin Mackenzie was at his bedside and wrote that a few moments before his death Clerk-Maxwell had said, 'God help me! God help my wife', and then turned to him and said, 'Colin, you are strong; lift me up.' He next said, 'Lay me down lower, for I am very low myself and it suits me to lie low'. After this he breathed deeply and slowly and with a long look at his wife passed away. He was buried beside his mother and father in Patron churchyard.

Detail
27.3 × 28 cm. Watercolour and white body colour on pale grey paper. Near Algiers. Inscribed 'From Nature'.

Tragically, Colin was to die but two years later, at the age of forty one. He died of apoplexy on board ship, a day out of Liverpool, and by his own request was buried beside George Wedderburn in the Dean cemetery in Edinburgh. A large crowd attended, but perhaps because of some whiff of scandal the Blackburns stayed away.

After Hugh's retirement life at Roshven became very quiet. Visitors were not an everyday occurrence, and the few that did arrive were usually family, neighbours, or occasionally ex-colleagues of Hugh's. Fleeming Jenkin, Professor of Engineering at Edinburgh (and a close friend of R. L. Stevenson), arrived one summer with his family who were introduced to a Roshven custom, kitchen dances. Jenkin took

to this so readily that, at the age of forty two, he began to learn the steps of the reel and introduced the custom to his own house. Visitors to Roshven had to adapt themselves to the fact that Hugh kept summer time, and consequently all the clocks were an hour ahead of the rest of the country.

Hugh and Jemima travelled extensively over the coming years, visiting Algeria, Spain, Italy, Sicily, Corfu, Greece, France, Germany and Switzerland. These tours were leisurely affairs, and in some cases seem to have had very little advance planning. They just stopped where and when the fancy took them and moved on when they had seen all they wished. Jemima drew anything and everything. Her ability to compose and paint crowds reached new heights, and on one occasion, in North Africa, she managed sixty six figures, six cattle and six horses on a piece of paper 20.5 cm by 30 cm, and yet still achieved an uncluttered look to her picture. She began increasingly to use coloured paper, usually a pale grey, and adopted the oil technique of underpainting in an opaque white and glazing a transparent colour over the top. When used sparingly, this gave startling and brilliant results.

At home, being landowners in the West Highlands was taking on a new significance. The public's conscience was becoming troubled by the plight of the crofters, and the Government of Westminster very slowly began to realise that the inhabitants of the Western Highlands and Islands were in severe difficulties. The ruthless depopulation forced on the area during the Highland Clearances, governmental indifference, and the extreme difficulty of transport, meant that the majority of people lived on or below the poverty line. The crofters complained of insecurity of tenure, frequent evictions, and excessive rents (often set by absentee landlords), and after ten years of poor harvests they eventually followed the Irish and rioted. The Battle of the Braes, which forced the Gladstone government to set up a commission of enquiry into the grievances of the crofters, took place in Skye in April 1882. Lord MacDonald's tenants protested at the loss of grazing rights, refused to pay their rent, and resisted eviction. A gunboat and a force of fifty Glasgow policemen were sent to the island to quell the riot; but this expeditionary force was met by a hundred men, women and children, and a pitched battle took place. A small group of crofters were taken prisoner and eventually fined in Inverness, but not without winning a moral victory.

On the mainland too feelings ran high. John MacDonald from Morvern, the neighbouring district to Moidart, wrote a fierce letter to the *Oban Times* in May 1882, suggesting that the owner of Drimnin estate should make some restitution to the farmers he had evicted 'as he is now in a manner reaping the benefit of their toil'. Although some disquiet was expressed in parts of Moidart, Roshven and Glenuig remained peaceful. The Blackburns were, after all, not grasping absentees, and they had chosen to build where as little disruption as possible would be caused to the local population. As landlords they were better than average. The estate shop has already been mentioned, nor was it the only indication that they cared for those living on the

Opposite above. Detail
23 × 28.5 cm. Watercolour. Bathing at Biarritz, painted during the Blackburn's 'Spanish Tour' of 1876.

Opposite below
24.7 × 28 cm. Watercolour and white body colour. April 1880. 'An Arab cemetery—Friday . . .'

estate and in the surrounding area. Jemima was known to nurse crofters, even those with contagious diseases, in their own homes; and when the local doctor could not cure some ailment she would write to a Dr Macleod in Glasgow seeking his advice. When the news of the Sudan War and the battle of Tel el Kebir became known, fearing for the safety of one of the local men who was serving in the Black Watch, she wrote to his Commanding Officer, and received the reply that he was alive and well and in receipt of the letter she had enclosed for him. The improvements to the estate had included the rebuilding and modernising of all their tenants' houses and the building of a new farm steading and mill, both of which provided employment for several men, while their wives as often as not worked in the house.

The Blackburns also set out to have the track which ran through the estate improved. As early as 1848 a Report to the Glasgow Committee on Destitution in the Highlands had commented that 'the bridlepath is not worthy of the name . . . parties travelling the route must pass on foot, or at some risk on horseback'. In 1859 they built a bridge over the Alisary burn at the eastern extremity of the estate, and where the bridle path ran on their land, widened it so that it was suitable for carts and wagons. They then set about persuading the Committee of the Lochaber District of Roads to undertake, firstly the repair of the rest of the path, and secondly the construction of a proper road. This was no small matter. The path was the major

Detail
15.8 × 16 cm. Watercolour. July 1859. Jemima helping Margaret to cross the Alisary burn. In the background can be seen the start of a bridge over the burn—the first stage in the improvement of the road.

Opposite. Detail
23.3 × 24.3 cm. Watercolour. Gathering bracken, which was used as bedding for the animals during the winter. On the banks of the Irine burn, Roshven.

route from Mull, Morven, Ardgour and Ardnamurchan to the north, and the only means of communication with the outside world for the inhabitants of Moidart. As Hugh pointed out in a long and persuasive letter, the population of the area was such that 'at Glenuig . . . there [was] a Schoolboard School with more than 50 scholars, and a Chapel seated for 300 at which the attendance is so great that there is (I am informed) frequently a crowd outside unable to gain admission.' In 1884 he published a memorial or petition which, despite being signed by every landowner and crofter in the district, received the reply that 'the statements therein are much exaggerated and the Highway a mere bridle path. The trustees having regard to the remoteness of the district and the steep and rocky nature of the country through which this highway passes and to the somewhat sparse population therein and consequent difficulty of getting suitable contractors have directed . . . that the proprietors of Roshven and Glenuig should themselves become the contractors for this road so far as it passes through their own estates.' This Hugh thought, not without reason, was the County ducking their responsibilities; and he pointed out that 'The road is a County Highway, I pay County rates and decline to keep in condition a road which ought to be kept out of the rates, and I have taken *every* means of making the County Trustees fulfill their trust with reference to it. Besides, not being a Radical, I have some consideration for the country folk and a desire that they should have their rights as well as the metropolitan shopkeepers of Fort William.'

It is perhaps some comment on the intransigent and dilatory nature of successive generations of Highland local government that Moidart eventually got its road in 1966, the population having dwindled from some two hundred and fifty to under forty.

While Hugh and Jemima were fighting a series of increasingly bitter skirmishes over the road, questions were beginning to be asked about a totally different form of transport. The Crofters Commission had reported unequivocally that lack of transport was at the heart of the problems of the West Highlands. A proposal to build a railway from Glasgow to Inverness up the west coast and through the Great Glen had been refused by Parliament in 1883, on the grounds that there was not enough traffic to warrant another railway in the Highlands. A line run by various companies already existed from Carlisle to Perth and on to Inverness. This meant that for the Blackburns to reach a railhead—at Kingussie—they would have to row five miles up the loch (this being easier with luggage than by the path) where on a Tuesday, Thursday or Saturday they could catch a coach to Fort William, thirty miles and six hours distant. From Fort William the mail coach departed every weekday at 6 am, reaching Kingussie at 12.20 if all went well.

In January 1889 the North British Railway Company proposed the West Highland line. They wished to leave the existing North British line at Helensburgh and proceed by Lochs Long and Lomond to Crianlarich, then up Strathfillan to Bridge of Orchy, from where they would strike out over the wild and barren Moor of Rannoch before dropping into Lochaber and approaching Fort William from the north. The line was to be concluded by taking it along the shore of Loch Eil and Loch Eilt, and then down Loch Ailort to a pier and terminus at Roshven.

The Blackburns first heard of these plans when on the morning of 2 November Margaret, while out for a walk, came across a young civil engineer, J. E. Harrison, surveying the ground to the north of the house and quite close to a small sandy bay the family used for bathing. She suggested that he should explain his presence to her father, who was justifiably annoyed to hear that a 'clandestine visit' had been made some weeks before by a Mr Forman, a Mr Macrae 'and company', when seemingly the plans had been formulated. Understandably he was upset and objected strongly; not however, as has been suggested, on the grounds of personal inconvenience. The Blackburns firmly believed that if the West Highlands were to prosper, and the wholesale emigration from the region be stopped, then transport would have to be improved. They felt, and set out to prove, that not only was the railway company wrong in its decision to terminate the line at Roshven but that if it were to go ahead it would be a mistake whose repercussions would be detrimental to the whole of the west coast. Hugh prepared the case in his usual quiet and methodical way. Plans, maps and charts were drawn up; photographs were taken of the proposed site and the planned structures so as to indicate the visual effect. He worked out how a breakwater would affect the tides of the loch, and therefore what the increase in pollution would be, calculating the breakwater's and proposed pier's length, breadth and cubic contents. He began to take meteorological notes, with particular reference to how gales affected the bay, and he contacted friends and colleagues to ask their expert opinion. When he appeared before a committee of the House of Lords, called to hear petitions against the bill, he was fully and totally prepared.

Initially the case seemed to go against him. Captain Swinburne and Mr J. Maclean (the proprietor of Glenuig) both gave evidence to the effect that Roshven was the best harbour in the area, while Hugh's case rested on the fact that it was no harbour at all. He pointed out that although the Admiralty chart marks Roshven as a good anchorage, the position in question was in the lee of a small island (Goat Island) some four hundred yards off shore, and not in the bay itself, explaining further that the sea between the anchorage and shore can get so rough that a vessel may have to wait a week before being able to land its passengers. He was questioned closely on the effectiveness of a pier and breakwater, and was able to demonstrate that neither would reach the anchorage, and further that the sea would wash over them at high tide and the parapet would disappear the first time there was a storm. Eventually the question of trade in the West Highlands was brought up.

Do you take any interest in the crofter question? *Yes.*

Or in developing the trade of the islands? *Yes.*

If this scheme, when executed, would be beneficial to them, you would hardly wish to stand in the way of it? *But I do not believe it would be a benefit to them.*

I said if it would? *If it should. If you will prove that like the 47th proposition of the First Book of Euclid.*

If I can demonstrate it like a proposition of Euclid then you will withdraw your opposition? *Yes.*

You do not want to stand in the way of a public improvement, I'm sure? *Certainly not.*

Sir William Thomson also testified to the inadequacy of the bay as an anchorage and to the uselessness of the proposed pier and breakwater—and adroitly avoided confusing his examiner and their Lordships with science when they persisted with questions on wave strength.

The petitioners won the day, and the line was terminated some twenty five miles further north, at Mallaig, from where a convenient ferry link could be established with Skye and the Outer Isles. In the closing years of the century the construction of the line brought dramatic changes to the village of Loch Ailort. Two thousand navvies were billeted there, a shop was opened, and the schoolhouse was turned into an eight-bed hospital. The contractor was Robert McAlpine of Glasgow, an enthusiast for the relatively new building medium of mass concrete; at the time the Mallaig railway extension became the greatest concentration of concrete construction in the world. Hugh, ever ready to experiment, used the technique in further additions to Roshven and in building a new house for his grieve. The line was opened on 1 April 1901, twelve years to the day since Hugh had presented his evidence to the House of Lords.

THE BLACKBURNS were very friendly with Annie Macleod, a daughter of Norman Macleod and a frequent visitor to Roshven. She was an enthusiastic folklorist and song collector, and collaborated with Harold Boulton in producing *Songs of the North.* Hugh, before the onset of deafness, had collected stories and songs from the local people of Moidart, particularly those with a bearing on the '45 Jacobite rising, and enjoyed the company of someone who shared this interest. She was popular also with William and Margaret, and could be relied upon to instigate a dance or concert at a moment's notice. In July 1882 Harold Boulton called at Roshven when returning from a holiday in Mull, and recalled the visit in a letter dated 1924:

> . . . From Oban I then took the steamer to Corpach and went by the post cart which started in the evening through Glenfinnan and down to Loch Ailort where I arrived in the very early morning. I then walked the remaining four miles to Roshven, the chief object of my journey being to discuss certain matters appertaining to *Songs of the North* with Miss A. C. Macleod who was staying with Professor and Mrs. Blackburn at that romantic spot. I arrive in time for breakfast and later the whole party went out picnicking, where we were joined by those very fine old Highlanders, the Macleans of Samalaman, who, I fear, have joined the majority long ago. Mrs. Blackburn was well known under

Detail
28.5 × 24.5 cm. Watercolour. 'Annie
MacLeod.' Anne C. MacLeod (1855–
1921), folk song collector, edited with
H. Boulton *Songs of The North* (1885).

the intitials of 'J.B.' as an artist and there is still a sketch at Roshven of the picnic party.

    While I was being rowed back in the evening down Loch
Ailort to catch the mail cart, the party were humming a scrap
of a shanty which Miss Macleod had picked up along the coast.
I did not learn till later that the original shanty had been added
to, and, so to speak, fetted up, but the words we sang it to as
we rowed down the loch were—

      Row us along, Roland and John
      Over the sea to Roshven.

    Having driven to Corpach and again thence by steamer
to Oban and thence by train to London I arrived at my Hertford-
shire home the following day there to learn that my father and
I had to start off on a business trip to Cologne the same evening.
Having crossed the Channel at night we proceeded on a tedious
railway journey to Cologne and though I had now been four
nights without sleeping in a bed I could not get to sleep in the
train because of the lilt of the Highland Boat Song and rattling
over the very noisy German lines the words of the Skye Boat
Song were forced upon me and fastened themselves on to the
all-compelling tune.

    They had in the meantime taken upon themselves a Jacobite
flavour, and introduced the familiar figure of Prince Charlie and
Flora MacDonald and 'Over the Sea to Roshven' had become
'Over the Sea to Skye'.

O let us sing and be glad ... while the sweet sunny hours may la
Time so one nough to be sad ... when the glories of Summer are

21 × 26 cm. Watercolour. September 1885. Left to right: J.M.T., ...?, ...?, J. Macleod, J.G., C.C., Alan (with pipe), Jemima, Annie MacLeod, Margaret (with dog), L.T., ...?, William, Hugh.

I remember very well that when I sent the words of the Skye Boat Song on to Miss Macleod and to our musical colleague, Malcolm Lawson, we agreed to use a phrase of Miss Macleod's to wrap the matter up as far as possible 'in the mists of antiquity'. We might have had less trouble subsequently as to infringement of copyright and other mental disturbances if even I had known, which I did not know till just before the War, that half of the tune owed its origin to the talent of Miss Macleod. Her modesty at the time forbade her to tell me that half of the tune was hers and only when I had to write and ask Lady Wilson (as she then was) for the exact facts, because of some controversy, did she give me the information.

For many years Jemima had been encouraged to produce a book detailing her methods of working, the landscape painter Peter Graham, a close friend, being particularly enthusiastic. *Instructions on Drawing by one who has experienced its difficulties* (1890) is characteristic in its gentle humour, modesty and good advice; but greater praise was reserved for her next publication.

'There are naturalists and naturalists. It is a pity that there are not more like Mrs Blackburn. This gifted lady belongs to the Gilbert White class.' Thus began a review of *Birds from Moidart* in the *Westminster Budget* on 10 January 1896. This was to be Jemima's last major work, and contrary to its title did not set out to illustrate every bird in Moidart, but 'only to represent such birds as I have known personally, and to add simply, and I trust truthfully, a few observations which I have had the opportunity of making on their life and habits'. The illustrations are, for the most part, those that appear in the 1868 edition of *Birds from Nature*, reduced in scale. Some of the later additions, presumably drawn specifically for the book, are inferior as she had begun to experience problems with her eyesight. A few of the plates that appear for the first time, however, were executed in the late '50s and early '60s and are of superb quality, notably the sparrowhawk, a magnificent freely painted study of a nightjar, and the head of a long-eared owl. Why it is that these were omitted from the earlier publications is hard to fathom. The text, is full of the most glorious anecdotal information and provides a neat, if modest, summation of a lifetime's work.

Both Colin Blackburn and Andrew Wedderburn died during 1896. Colin had had a distinguished career. After being called to the Bar in 1838 he had been appointed Justice of the Queen's Bench and knighted in 1860, then in 1876 raised to the peerage. Andrew, Jemima's most loved brother, had retired from the Indian Civil Service in 1878, and the following year, after the death of James Clerk-Maxwell, had inherited Glenlair. His death in Bath on 12 May caused Jemima considerable grief, the news taking some time to reach her as she and Hugh were travelling in Italy at the time.

Hugh was by now almost totally deaf. Jemima's eyesight caused her increasing difficulties and she too complained that she had to sit close to anyone speaking in order to hear all that was said. These infirmities strengthened, if anything the affection that they held for each other and the delight they experienced in travelling abroad together. In 1897 they planned a final tour, and set out in the *Lusitania* on a cruise that would enable them to revisit many of their favourite places in the Mediterranean.

For some years friends had tried to persuade Jemima to write her memoirs and in 1899 she made a somewhat desultory start. Her handwriting had never been good but, hindered by her failing sight, it degenerated into a vaguely patterned scrawl. She wrote well and logically in a fresh and idiosyncratic style until, after some thirty sheets of foolscap, it becomes clear that she was working to no set plan. Her narrative drifts, rambles and stops. Sometime after 1900 Hugh made a chronology from the sketchbooks and seems to have persuaded her

Detail
28.8 × 24.5 cm. 'Hugh.' June 1889.

17.5 × 28.5 cm. Watercolour. 2 July
1863. Hugh chasing ponies from the
croquet lawn in front of Roshven House
at 4 o'clock in the morning.

to start again, using it as a skeleton on which to build. He then correc-
ted and annotated her manuscript.

The memoirs as presented here are an amalgamation of both versions, with notes to identify people, places and incidents mentioned
in the text. Hugh's corrections are identified by the phrase 'HB's
notes'. The two versions differ little, often only in details remembered
and adjectives used. Both omit much: little mention is made of her
ornithological work, her painting or Hugh's photography; and both
have little to say about the period after 1870. However, when they
are considered in conjunction with her paintings, we can see each
aspect of her work pulling the other into focus and providing a clear,
unique and mildly humorous view of life.

Detail
17.5 × 14 cm. Watercolour and body
colour on grey paper. *c.* 1860. Hugh and
William reading in the drawing room
at Roshven.

Sea Eagle's Nest

22.5 × 16.5 cm. Ink drawing. 20 June
1863. Jemima being shown a sea-eagles
nest at Inver Aylort [sic].

21 × 29 cm. Watercolour. June 1865.
Carting the peats, Roshven.

June 1865

18 × 25.3 cm. Watercolour. 1864. The Blackburn family skating at Killearn. Left to right: Rebbeca (Menie) Blackburn, Jean Blackburn, Andy Blackburn (1851–87), Helen Blackburn (1851–1929), (Nancy), Margaret, G.R., Isabella Blackburn (Pam), Jemima, . . .?, . . .?, . . .?, . . .?, . . .?

MEMOIRS

MY BIRTH was in sorrow, and I think it left in me a gloomy and stormy disposition, more inclined to the pleasures of memory than those of hope. I was born on 1 May 1823 in 31 Heriot Row, Edinburgh. My father died six months before I was born, at the age of forty, in consequence of catching a severe chill on a journey to St Mary's Isle to do business with his sister Lady Selkirk. The chill took the form of congestion of the brain, and after a few days' unconsciousness he died, to the great grief of all his friends. He was Solicitor-General for Scotland and expected to have been raised to the Bench. He was very handsome, with beautiful dark eyes with a steady penetrating look which was said to have an effect on the witnesses in law cases of making them afraid to tell lies. I have seen a letter from his great friend Lord Meadowbank describing him, saying that his striking quality was integrity. Old friends of my father used to say, when I was a child, that I resembled him in appearance, which I was pleased to hear. If I had had a choice in the matter I would fain have delayed his death till I could have known him.

There is a beautiful portrait of my father by Raeburn, now at Killearn—also one of my mother—his last and unfinished. It was interrupted by the birth of my elder sister, and Raeburn died before he was able to complete it. My mother, who was one of the Clerks of Penicuik, had naturally a very cheerful disposition but was subject to fits of depression when ill. She was very pretty with blue eyes and used to be much named 'the Daisy of Pentland'.

My father bought our house in Heriot Row soon after it was built. It was a large house five stories high. The sun shone brightly in it, but so much so as to blister the paint on our windows and make the venetian blinds smell bad. It had a hot bath in it, a rarity at that time, a great leaden thing generally with 'black clocks'[1] floating in it, of primitive construction, and requiring a boiler to be heated by a big fire in the laundry half a storey underground. It was not a thing of everyday use. Every Friday we girls were scrubbed in it with yellow soap, every Saturday the boys, from top to toe. I do not remember a bath in any of the big country houses I used to visit. There was one, a tin thing lying aside at Craigflower[2] in case of illness, but I

1. Black beetles.

2. Estate and mansion near Torryburn, Fife. Property of Jemima's uncle, Andrew Wedderburn-Colvile.

Detail
18 × 25 cm. Watercolour. Baby Gull.
Frontispiece to Part 11 of *Birds from
Nature*, 1868.

never saw it used. People in those days did their cleanliness in clothes, not in their skins.

Many years afterwards when flannel shirts came into fashion it was otherwise. In those times the allowance was two clean shirts a day, one in the morning, another at dinner time, always linen. Also washable caps were worn under our bonnets. It would have been thought very dirty to wear a hat or bonnet with the same lining for months. The dress worn by young girls at that date consisted of short petticoats, cotton trousers with frills. It was very comfortable and permitted us climbing trees. Some less favoured young people were put in long petticoats and bonnets. We generally wore pink cotton shady bonnets called 'shearers'. We had cotton stockings, sometimes fine thread openwork ones—very fit for letting in the midges. I remember the horror of my first pair of worsted stockings and how they tickled me. I never wore worsted underthings till I was in Switzerland walking in the glaciers; everybody does so now. The doctors advised cotton underclothing in preference to linen for young people.

One of my first recollections was upsetting some scalding porridge on my arm and burning it severely; also having a doll's house given to me. I always hated dolls, so kept a pet stumpy blue pigeon in it called Dobbin, whose mission in life seemed to be to eat. I have never since been without tame pigeons.

We had a Scotch nurse, a very pious sabbatarian old woman whom we called 'Mam'. My mother was not sabbatarian and allowed me to draw or cut out beasts in paper on Sundays, but Mam would not allow one to paint. Such are the distinctions in such matters. She objected to our whistling for the dogs on Sundays; we might only chirp to them or call by their names. We were not allowed to make a noise on Sunday or play at noisy games. I composed a hymn:

> He who plays at ninepins shall
> On Sunday surely go to hell
> From ninepins guard our hearts O Lord
> And keep us quiet with our dolls.

My mother's family were Presbyterians, my father's Episcopalians. I found the former dull and so chose to frequent the latter. In St Paul's Chapel, Edinburgh there was a painted glass window, not in the first rank as the connoisseurs said, but to see it was impressive. It was full of dark clouds with a bright red cross in the middle. It was changed afterwards for one full of saints and apostles of the conventional kind, which did not interest me at all.

I was not religious and believed in nothing. I thought religion to be all got up for women and children, as men did not go to church often unless taken there by women. At a country house I stayed at, we girls were kept in on Sunday afternoons for reading, while the men and the boys all went out for a walk with the dogs.

I often wished I had been born a beast or a bird to roam about freely out of doors and have no responsibility and never have to think. I used to be much bothered by thinking, especially of impossible things such as infinite space, and time having no beginning and no end, till my head felt like bursting.

I was always ill up to ten years of age and had horrible dreams and nightmares, fancying that an old dead carthorse's head with hanging lips was looking at me through the bed curtains, and sometimes that a pig pursued me upstairs and from room to room, and just as I was shutting the door against it, thrust its snout through till I woke with a yell. Old Mam was a kind good sort of person but injudicious in her treatment. I must have been troublesome when unable to go to sleep and she used to tell me that there was a woman without a head that went about the house at night, and to enforce her words tapped on the bedstead. It was her only fault. I wept when she died as I have never wept since.

My mother told me always to say my prayers at night and I did so in a perfunctory manner becaues I did not like to break my word.

When I was aged about two and very delicate, our doctor's treatment was very unlike that at present. He had my head shaved and constantly had leeches put on my temples. How well I remember their bites and the heavy way they flopped down on my cheek when they were full. After they were stripped, salt was applied to their sides and they vomited forth much blood (I was quite used to the sight of blood and have never minded it, whch is rather convenient in case of an accident). After they were stripped and salted I kept them to make pets out of, but they seldom lived long.

12.5 × 21.8 cm. A monochrome study for an engraving possibly illustrating a German fairy tale.

3. John Abercrombie (1780–1844), Physician-in-ordinary to the King.

4. (1757–1839), author of Essay on *Nature and Principles of Taste* (1790).

When I was about four years old the great consulting physician Dr Abercromby[3] was called in. I remember him as a grey haired little man with a kind manner. He found me in bed cutting out paper shapes of animals. He said I was not to do any lessons and that drawing would be a good amusement for me, so he drew on a scrap of note paper a house of the conventional type, with a chimney at each end and a window at each side and a door in the middle. I was to copy it before his next visit. I did so and surrounded it with horses, cows and all manner of beasts. I wish the good doctor's drawing had been preserved—that was the beginning of my drawing and I have gone on with it. I was given much encouragement from Archibald Alison,[4] clergyman of St Paul's—then bedridden and nearing his end. He had long grey hair and beautiful fine features and had written a book about beauty (not much read now and which I have never read). He told me I had a talent given me for drawing and that I must go on with it and improve it. I have never forgotten him or his words.

There is much written and spoken about the joys of childhood I never experienced. People used to call me 'baby' which I did not like, and kissed me which I liked worse, and hugged me which was worst of all. It is a great mistake to treat children so. It is best to let them make the first advances. People were all very kind to me however, and some rich old ladies, the Jeffrey sisters and the Miss Aytouns, used to take me out drives. I enjoyed watching the horses trotting along but wondered how on earth one could ever draw their legs as they changed their shape at every movement. The carriages then had front windows and were built with C springs, and occasionally made children sick when sitting back to the horses. They were driven by a postillion. I used to have to talk properly to my old companions—I used to unfold my mind to them but when I found they reported my sayings to my mother I gave that up. I used to dislike very much when the old ladies called me 'a little artist'.

We used to hear horrid stories in our nursery after the murders committed by Burke and Hare. Dead bodies were much wanted for the anatomists to use in training their pupils, and these were expensive and difficult to get. A sort of people called body snatchers or resurrectionists used to dig the corpses out of their graves and sell them for that purpose, so iron rails were put over the graves to protect them. I hate the sight of railings about graves. The practice is continued yet though no longer necessary for that purpose. Servants used to object much to being sent to hospitals as they supposed that after death their bodies would be used for dissection. Burke and Hare used to murder people that they thought would not be missed, to supply the want, and it was said that some bodies were brought in warm and that might have been resuscitated. It was found out by a corpse of an idiot called 'daft Jamie' who had some recognisable peculiarity in his great toe, which was known. Many of my schoolboy friends and young students attended the hanging of Burke (I forget if Hare was hanged as he turned King's evidence) but Burke was, and skinned too. I remember my teacher offering me a present of a piece of the skin as I had done my lessons well. I declined it with thanks.

There were not many children's books in my young days. I learned to read somehow. I remember my mother reading Barbauld's[5] 'Come hither, Charles' with me and pointing with a pin to the letters. I could write text very well, better than I have done since though I do not remember how I came to do so. I wrote stories with illustrations or rather illustrations with stories.

I attended classes at a very respectable old lady's house in our street when I was well enough to do so. She was pompous. My first lesson was to learn a dozen words in the dictionary by heart. I remember her writing a note to my mother and dating it 3 o'clock M.P. She overlooked our French exercises. One day the French master looking at mine asked why I had made an alteration. I did not tell him it was she who had made it. The girls were as a rule rather stupid. I made some friends among them but they were not so good to play with as the boys. I only began to realise that I was not a boy when I had to wear long dresses. I and another girl were good runners so played with them at tig or prisoners' base, trap ball, and a childish sort of cricket. They were all active games as I had got healthy then, and have been ever since, all these long years.

My principal friend was a Miss Purdie, daughter of an important music seller.[6] Shortly before we left school, she asked me to take a walk with her in the garden and said she would now take leave of me as it would not do for us to continue our acquaintance. I could not think why, but she said we belonged to different circles. I remonstrated but she was firm, so that was the last I saw of her.

I used to sit out and read in the front garden on fine days if we were in town in the summer. My favourite book was *Heathen Mythology*, written by a lady for her daughters that they might understand allusions in poetry—I drew pictures of the characters with no clothes on them which I gave to my companions. Another book was *True Stories of Ancient History*, with pictures—the one I admired most was Curtius leaping into the chasm on a beautiful white horse with a long mane. When I was in Rome long afterwards I looked for the place but found only a ditch. We had a lot of old fashioned books in the house. Among others was the *British Poets* which I looked into but did not get much good from; nor did I admire them at all. Most of them were improper and others twaddly. Cowper's opinion that in winter 'female feet too weak to struggle with tenacious clay were best at home', did not suit my taste. On a fine winter's day I preferred to go out with the shooters on the clay soil of Killearn and could cross a ploughed field as well as they could, and liked it better than sitting on the sofa at home.

I did not like poetry except Milton, Shakespeare and Scott. Afterwards when the Waverley novels were available to me I cared for nothing else and when I had read them once I read them again, till I got rather mixed among them. They were favourite subjects for illustrations. About the age of ten I read Paley's *Natural Theology* and was much impressed by it (I wonder now what effect Darwin would have had). I was also captivated by Sir Charles Bell's Bridge-water treatise on *The Hand*. I was always very fond of anatomy and

5. Mrs Barbauld (1748–1825), poet, essayist, educational writer. *Lessons for Children, Hymns in Prose for Children.*

6. Est. 1804 at 85 Princes Street, still trading in 1855.

used to get dead mice to skin and find out how their muscles acted.

My favourite toy was a Noah's Ark. In my first one the horses' tails were docked. It was the fashion then; afterwards it went out. Race horses were never docked, nor hunters. In recent years the practice went out, so much so that horses for cavalry with docked tails were not allowed, unless in times of scarcity when others were not to be had. Clydesdale horses for Germany or America always had their tails left on, as they did in this country; but now I am sorry to say they are cut as short as possible and look very ugly and indecent.

One of my early recollections was the passing of the Reform Bill in 1832. There was a great rejoicing among the radicals. An order or a request, I don't know which, was announced for an illumination of the houses. A riot was expected and the Yeomanry were called out. I remember the clattering of the horses' hoofs when our neighbour, young Dundas, went off after dark to join the troops' rendezvous at the riding school. Soon the streets were filled with men in light brown fustian with torches in their hands, shouting and throwing stones at our windows as we would not light them up. They soon smashed all the windows and then began hammering on the door. It was rather an awful sight but though much excited I did not feel afraid, only fierce, and paced about the house with the sword belonging to my father's court dress; and I am sure if the mob had broken in I would have stuck some of them, or at least tried to do so. We could see them well from our nursery window which was high up above the reach of the stones. All the other windows in the front of the house were smashed, and a comfortless state we were in for some days, as glaziers were not to be had. The only thing that escaped was a white plaster horse on the lunette above the door; afterwards we called him the Duke of Wellington. The three middle, and highest, houses in Heriot Row belonged to Sir R. Dundas of Dunira, my mother, and Mr Fergusson of Trochrigg, all Tories. Ours was thought to belong to my uncle, Sir G. Clerk of Penicuik, who had for long been Tory M.P. for Midlothian, as he used to be much there; so it was specially attacked.

When political opinions rose high there was much speechifying about the streets. Our neighbour Mr Aytoun held forth from his drawing room window and John Dalrymple, Lord Stair, from the top of a blue and yellow bus. We thought he looked like a puggy on a band box. (Buses were new inventions then.) Country gentlemen of different politics did not associate with one another at all. You would never meet a Whig at a Tory house or vice versa. Even our tradesmen were chosen for their politics, not for their skill or the goodness of their wares. Thank heavens it is not so now.

When I was old enough not to have to sleep with my mother I was given a garret on the top of the house, with a good big window opening on to the roof. I used to go out and see the sunrise over the Calton Hill, and sit out at night and smoke with my brother Andrew and discuss the ball we had been to.

When I was about fifteen and staying at Killearn, Colin Blackburn, afterwards the Judge, used to take me and my sister-in-law Helen

Opposite
25 × 17.5 cm. Watercolour. A bonfire in the narrow, winding and picturesque ravine known as Ash Dhu, near Killearn House.

17.8 × 25.5 cm. Watercolour. 1871.
Women waulking cloth—watched by a
Roshven house party.

9.5 × 14.3 cm. Andrew Wedderburn and Jemima sitting on the leads at Heriot Row, discussing a ball they had attended earlier in the evening.

7. Edward B. Ramsay (1793–1872), Dean of Edinburgh 1841. Author of *Reminiscences* (1858).

8. Henry H. Hilman (1791–1868), Dean of St Paul's 1849.

Blackburn out on scrambling walks over the hills and through the burns. When they were deep he used to take us up, one under each arm, and carry us through them. He talked history to us in an interesting and rational manner, tracing the progress of public opinion in the different countries of Europe. It was much more interesting than sitting through Hume's *History of England* at thirty pages a day. I began to like it.

One of my great clergyman friends was Dean Ramsay,[7] an excellent, most lovable man, a good preacher and the most beautiful reader of the prayers, much beloved by his congregation at St John's and the Sunday School children. One seldom hears the prayers well read now that intoning has come in. Bishop Tissot was another friend. A fine reader and a good preacher too, he was at St Paul's. I met him once at Penicuik House in company with Dean Milman,[8] who asked him about the inhabitants of Edinburgh. He said 'We are all doctors, lawyers, schoolmasters and clergymen, too many of us for all the good we do.' At an evening party when clairvoyance, table turnings, and spirit rappings were rife, an old lady who was sitting talking to him asked if he did not think the devil was in it? 'Madam', he said, 'I should be only too glad to think so, for then I should know that the devil was in his dotage.' He admired nature in pictures. We sometimes went to the picture exhibitions together; one might almost have thought that the chief purpose of scenery was to be painted, as he also said that water was not made for drinking but for making drink of. I used to visit him when he was old and had to give up work, and have long talks with him. In those days there used to be three pulpits in the church or chapel, as he called the Episcopal place of worship, in distinguishment from the Established. The highest was for preaching, the middle for reading prayers, and the lowest for the clerk who did the responses. Preaching was always done in a black silk gown—when surplices were worn in preaching it was considered a Popish innovation.

Mrs Alison, daughter-in-law to the old clergyman, lived in the same street as us and was a great friend of mine though much older than I. She was a cultured, refined charming person. I often visited her and we had long talks on abstruse subjects. Both she and her husband were very hospitable and had eminent people at their parties. Dr Alison was a very distinguished consulting physician. He was a most amiable man and bestowed a great deal of his time and skill on the very poor, however ungrateful. One day he was visiting in the slums he laid down his hat, and when he was leaving found another of the vilest description put in its place—he only laughed.

A young medical student, Henry Ackland[9] lodged with them. I used to get him frogs and hedgehogs to study. He was afterwards Sir Henry and Professor of Anatomy at Oxford where we visited him many years after. Mrs Alison introduced me to Professor Goodsir,[10] the anatomist, and by this means I got in to see the Surgeons' Museum where the skeleton of Eclipse, the great racehorse, was kept. Burke's skeleton was there too—a short thick-set man. Some years afterwards Professor Goodsir was teaching his students the anatomy of the horse, and remembering my taste for horses gave me private lessons in the college. My uncle John Clerk-Maxwell used to accompany me. I made drawings from the anatomies, then made sketches of horses in various attitudes with muscles coloured to show the action. I submitted these to my teacher who approved.

Uncle John was a great favourite of mine—he was always very kind to me. The best book I had was given to me by my Grand Aunt Mary (Lady Clerk); it was a handsome copy of Bewick's land birds, and he used to take me on his knee and tell me stories about the tail-pieces. He was the most sensible and kind man possible and thought out everything so as to act with judiciosity—a favourite word of his. While driving himself about in his little carriage which he called the 'hurley' he always let the horse get over the top of the hill before he set it trotting again, thereby saving it much labour at little expense of time. He was very fond of beasts and kind to them, never grudging a feed of corn to his friends' horses that rested in his stable for, he said, 'no one grudged a glass of wine to a friend, and a feed of corn cost less'. One year when my mother was not well we wintered with Uncle John at Glenlair. I used to take long winter walks with him along the muddy roads. His conversation was very instructive and I liked it very much. I went out with him when he was shooting; he was a fair shot but never fired at anything that he was not likely to hit and shoot dead. It was a great country for pigs; he asked me if I would like to see them killed but I declined.

After the death of his wife Uncle John and his son James came

9. Sir Henry Ackland (1815–1900), Professor of Clinical Medicine, Oxford 1851. Close friend of Ruskin.

10. John Goodsir (1814–67), Curator, College of Surgeons 1841. Professor of Anatomy 1846.

to live with us in Heriot Row. James went to Cambridge on the advice of Lord Kelvin and Hugh Blackburn, and was highly distinguished there for his mathematics. He had a great turn that way when quite a young boy. He made an invention for drawing ovals with pins and string which was thought ingenious. Professor James Forbes was shown it, and the British Association in Edinburgh. He and I used to construct mechanical toys together, jumping jacks and wheels of life. I made the drawings of animals in motion for them, and was pleased to discover when the instantaneous photography came in that I got all the motions correct, except once only. I made a mistake in the legs of a galloping horse; it gallops differently from a dog in an accelerated canter, not in a succession of leaps.

James became a Professor at Aberdeen (Marischal College), and married a daughter of Principal Dewar there. This did not give much satisfaction to his friends and relations. The lady was neither pretty, nor healthy, nor agreeable, but much enamoured of him. It was said that her sister had brought about the match by telling him how much she was in love with him, and he being of a very affectionate tender disposition married her out of gratitude. Her mind afterwards became unsettled but he was always most kind to her, and put up with it all. She alienated him from his friends and was of a suspicious and jealous nature. He died of cancer, as his mother had done, and suffered much with great patience. He was truly religious and had the sweetest temper of any man I ever knew. I do not think I ever saw him angry or heard him say a word against any one. His widow published a life of him written by the Revd. Lewis Campbell, an early friend and neighbour of his in Edinburgh. Of course under these circumstances the history of his married life could not be entered into. All this took place after his father's death.

I have a pleasing recollection of a last visit from Uncle John in the College of Glasgow. He was then in bad health and we had to send for a doctor in the middle of the night. It was a short visit but he feared he had been of trouble to us, which I assured him he had not. I was very glad to have him. We had a very affectionate parting and I never saw him again.

There were many clever old ladies in Edinburgh whom I used to visit, principally my Grand Aunt, Miss Margaret Blackburn. We used to adjourn to her flat in Castle Street after church on Sundays. On her table were laid out sticks of barley sugar on white paper and hard sea biscuits (for which the bakers in Leith were famous). I never ate lunch in those days; we breakfasted about nine and dined at five or six, eating nothing in between. I thought it effeminate to want anything to eat after a good breakfast. My mother used to eat a little biscuit and drink a glass of water. We used to have tea and toast about eight.

My Aunt was an interesting character, a remarkably clever old lady, a great politician and a strong Tory. She had a wonderful memory and could repeat long screeds from books she had read, though she had not read many as there were not many to read then. She knew a lot of history; I suppose Hume was the great authority. She read

Opposite. Above
12 × 21.1 cm. Watercolour. James Clerk-Maxwell and his father with Jemima running to shelter from rain.

Opposite. Below
21 cm dia. One of several phenakistoscope wheels made by James Clerk-Maxwell and painted by Jemima. Collection. The Natural Philosophy Museum, University of Aberdeen.

18.7 × 17 cm. 'Common Guillemot.'
Birds from Nature (1862) pl. IV.
Birds from Nature (1868), pl. IV.
Birds from Moidart, p. 161.

11. Fourth son of John Blackburn,
banker in Edinburgh.

Shakespeare and the British poets, and the novels of the day—she
could repeat whole pages of *Tom Jones*. She liked having children
about her and watched their ways and appreciated those who could
converse. She had many visitors, a good many of them young men
who enjoyed an argument with her. I remember at the time of the
Reform agitation, when the mob used to throw stones at the coaches
of the gentry and nobility, Andrew Blackburn[11] maintaining that it
was no worse to throw a stone at the Duchess of Buccleuch than at
any other woman. This made Aunt Margaret furious. At the end of
it Andrew said, 'We are all fallible mortals.' 'Fallible mortals!' said
she, 'you are a cavilling doit!'

She used to have Saturday dinner parties for the tribe of young
cousins. Among the delicacies she served were stewed oysters (which
used to be common then), 'partans' (crabs) which were large and fine
in Edinburgh, and delicious strawberry jam. I remember her before
she broke a leg, walking about in the Queen Street gardens opposite
her house, in a gigantic straw bonnet shaped like a coal scuttle. She
was always rather blind and used to have a reader, for she liked to
know what was in the newspapers. She would sit knitting in her old
fashioned armchair with a large green shade over her eyes. She had
a very high long nose like the Duke of Wellington's, and a thin deter-

mined looking mouth with a small but not receding chin (the Duke's chin was even more remarkable than his nose). She was much missed when she died. She had a small competency which she left to my cousins the Miss Colviles, and her books to John Ogilvy. She did not leave me anything. She said to my mother I could do very well without it.

The old ladies used to speak Scotch in these days, more so than servants do now, but it was very ladylike and pretty.

I had two other old aunts who also lived in a flat while they were in Edinburgh. They were John Irving's half sisters, not so clever as Aunty, but also speaking Scotch. They were fond of telling stories and struggled for which of them was to tell it. Jeanie, the elder, had the longest breath and when Mary found herself defeated she spent her last breath with a long 'whew' of a whistle and gave up.

Late in life they rented Lord Newton's place at the source of the Clyde, a sheep farm in a wild part of Lanarkshire. We visited them in the summer. I used to go wandering about the hills finding insects which I carried home in a box and generally found that they had devoured each other. On rainy days I copied woodcuts out of the *Penny Magazine* (the only publication of its kind then). The elder ones played cribbage in the evenings.

I used to draw the cows in the byre from nature. Some of the workmen took a look at what I was doing in passing. On finding me still at work an hour or two afterwards they said, 'It's an unco' tediesome thing, the drawing!'

I used to fraternise with a little herd girl sometimes. She did not admire Newton. She told me she came from 'the village of Penicuik, a beautiful place where there were houses on both sides of the road for a mile.' At Newton there was nothing to be seen except when the Glasgow to Carlisle coach passed. I have almost always found that that class of people prefer town to country and do not admire the beauties of nature much—if at all.

My mother used to write long letters to the Aunties with all the Edinburgh gossip she could collect, and they wrote long answers which they called 'echoes' as they had nothing new to tell. They always sent a present of cheese with their letters.

They had a brother, John Irving, who was in youth a great friend of Sir Walter Scott. As boys they sat on Arthur's Seat, about the Salisbury Crag, and told each other stories. Scott used to say that Irving told the best of the two. (I remember one day standing by the drawing-room window in Heriot Row with our tame turtle doves on my shoulders to show Sir Walter Scott, who was driving past—the outside of his coach was all I saw of him.) John Irving became a man of business and a Writer to the Signet; he seemed to me to be a prosy sort of old person. He was always very busy as a 'rod' trustee. He had a high collar to his coat and long black tails and so much resembled a rook that we used to call rooks 'rod trustees'. He retained a love of romance and was much interested when I told him I was going to take some lessons in Italian, and sent me a copy of *Orlando Furioso*. He was pretty well off and kept a little carriage. He wanted a new

12. James H. Mackenzie (1810–65), m.(1) Janet Wedderburn 1888, (2) Jane Norton. Lawyer in Edinburgh.

13. Sailed for New South Wales 17 July 1887 in *Portland* ex Greenock.

14. Sailed 17 May 1845 in *Terror* ex Greenhithe.

15. John Irving's grave was discovered at Point Victory on 25 September 1880 by a Lt. Schwatha. The grave contained parts of a skeleton, the remains of a uniform, some canvas, which had been sewn together round the body, a silk handkerchief, and a lens. A medal, which had apparently been discovered by the Eskimos, lay on the grave. The bones were removed and taken to the United States, whence they were carried across the Atlantic on board the *S.S. Circassia* by invitation of the Anchor Line. They were interred with full naval honours on 7 January 1881.

horse for it so my brother George looked one out for him. He and James Mackenzie[12] went out with him one day to try it. The horse edged at something and backed; the young men promptly jumped out of the carriage; but he sat still with his glass at his eye and calmly remarked to the horse, 'I hae na bought ye yet'. When he was telling a story he always acted it or gesticulated. One day at dinner he was describing the resurrectionists and how they worked themselves into the graves. He dug and burrowed with his hands till he nearly disappeared under the table.

John Irving had a large family, one daughter and several sons. I did not care for any of them except John the sailor. After serving for some time in the navy and as there was nothing particular going on, he went to Australia.[13] At this time young and old were interested in Arctic exploration and when he returned to this country he joined the Franklin expedition.[14] I can not remember whether he sailed on the *Erebus* or the *Terror*. He came to see us at Killearn before he started. He had been in the Arctic regions before and was frost bitten which twisted his upper lip, but otherwise he was good looking and very dark. He talked for ever of Australia and told me he had eaten parrots. I asked what they tasted like but he could only tell me 'they had a parroty taste'. I never saw him again. He wrote to his father from Shetland, after which he was never more heard of. A party in search of Franklin some years after found some property of his, silver spoons with his crest and an Edinburgh Academy medal. They were brought home and exhibited in the Fisheries Exhibition in London. His body was found long after and sent home; he was buried in the Dean cemetery after a very fine funeral.[15]

I did not care for society in my youth nor did I look forward to 'coming out' though I enjoyed juvenile dancing parties. I loved dancing. My teacher was an English opera dancer married to a Frenchman. I was, I think, one of her favourite pupils as I was small and active. She was very unfair to the well grown and awkward girls and made them cry. I used to try to imitate her in an exaggerated manner, bounding across the room with great leaps; she seemed rather pleased.

My ball dresses used to be of good Indian white muslin, sometimes trimmed with a pattern in white or in colours; they were generally given to me by my Aunt, Mrs Colvile, who encouraged the industry in the village of Torryburn. They were of a length to show the feet, so good dancing could be appreciated. Before my first ball, in the Assembly Rooms, I had to get a wreath for my head as was worn at that time. My mother told the milliner that as I was small she wanted something plain and simple. 'Ah yes', said the milliner with a sigh, 'poor thing, something not to attract observation.' I certainly did not attract observation; the only person who asked to be introduced to me was a Mr Johnstone of Alva, a middle aged man. We danced; he said I looked as if I should say something good 'but it never came'. He afterwards visited at Craigflower when I was there. My Aunt, an enthusiast in matrimony, encouraged his visits—without result!

In my youth the hideousness of dress was a great grievance. How

Detail
12.8 × 15.5 cm. Watercolour. Van Amburgh, the American lion tamer, much admired by Queen Victoria, the Duke of Wellington and Landseer. Drawn on a visit to Edinburgh with Andrew Ducrow's circus in 1840.

one admired, at a fancy ball, an old fashioned costume or a foreign one. The arrangement of hair was frightful; it was divided in the middle. Bunches of ringlets hanging down the cheeks was 'front hair', and the 'back hair' was drawn up tight into a 'tapie tourie' on the top of the head. Front and back hair were considered as separate parts of the body, as much so as eyes and noses. I have heard of an old bachelor who, when asked why he never married, replied that he had 'never seen the scruff of the neck that he could like'. Bonnets followed the shape of the coiffure, from the coal scuttle bonnet diminishing from year to year till it became in time a little bunch of lace with an artificial flower in it, barely covering the head, and called by wags a 'come kiss me quick'. It hardly felt decent, especially in church.

When Charles Kean[16] came to Edinburgh, when he first became famous, and acted at the theatre, then my mother used to take a box and we went to it very often. *Macbeth* was my first Shakespeare play. I knew it almost by heart and enjoyed it immensely. Kean acted very much looking at our box; he was not handsome but had a fine eye, and spoke and walked well. I saw him in various characters and remember him perfectly still. I think him the best actor I ever saw either in tragedy or comedy. Lord Meadowbank liked him very much and on an 'off day' asked him to dinner, and we young people were asked in the evening. He took a great deal of notice of me, and having seen some of my drawings called me a 'Landseer in petticoats'. I adored him. That evening he enacted, with his shirt collar turned down, a shipwreck from Byron. I wanted to read it afterwards but could not find it in my copy of the poems. While staying with a young lady friend in the country I took up a complete copy of Byron's poems and found it in *Don Juan*. I used to visit Kean and his wife Ellen

16. Charles Kean (?1811–68), son of Edmund Kean, played Young Norval 1827, Richard III 1830, and other Shakespearean roles. First appeared in Edinburgh 1837.

Tree when they came to Glasgow. They did Shakespeare mostly, as Irving has done since, but had not such elaborate scenery.

We had some very good actors at the Edinburgh Theatre Royal long ago. Murray, humorous and pathetic beyond any I have seen. His Grandfather Whitehead was most affecting; he also did Falstaff very well. The first play I ever saw was *Paul Pry* in which he took the lead part. We had also Mackay as Bailie Nichol Jarvie, and Loyd and another good looking young man whose name I forget, who did all the young heroes. He also taught watercolour drawing. He was supposed to be a gentleman in reduced circumstances who had married early and had to work for his livelihood.

I spent a good deal of my time with my father's sister, Lady Selkirk, at St Mary's Isle. She had been in Canada with her husband who was a man before his time. He wished to help the Highland emigrants who had been driven from their homes to make way for sheep. There was no one to take care of them in Canada and they were in great danger from the fur hunters who wished to get rid of them, as settlers interfered with their trade. He went to the West Highlands and collected emigrants with the help of Macdonald of Arisaig in 1811. He founded Manitoba but was much persecuted by the Hudson Bay Company, a north-west company of fur traders. My cousin, Lady Katherine Douglas, was born in Canada though her sister Isabella was not. When they went abroad they took with them a girl from Kirkcudbright who remained serving them all her life, becoming housekeeper at last. She was a dear old woman. We used to have afternoon tea in her room, as did the shooters in the winter afternoons (though the present style of afternoon tea had not yet been invented). Lord Selkirk became consumptive on his return from Canada and he died on a visit to Pau in 1822.

Aunt Selkirk became very deaf owing, I believe, to the cold of Canada. She used to read the Waverley novels to Lady Katherine and me. She also played music very well, especially Scotch, for her own amusement when we stayed out late in the winter afternoons and she began to feel anxious about us. When shown a new piece she would read it over and say if she thought it pretty. I remember once when she was playing the organ to us, the young gentleman who was at the bellows stopped blowing for some reason, and she carried on playing all the same. I remember her playing of Pergolesi's 'Gloria in excelsis'; it was beautifully expressive. Aunt Selkirk was brought up an Episcopalian but thought it right when in Scotland to attend the Established church. In England she always went to the Episcopalian church and used the prayer book in her private devotions. At Kirkcudbright church the minister furnished her with a list of psalms, chapters of the Bible etc. that she might join in the worship. When the high church manner prevailed most of the young people refused to go to the Presbyterian church, though their parents continued to go there. She was fond of travelling both by sea and by land. She took us on a tour in England; we sailed to Exeter and then went in open carriages.

Some of my friends and relations went to the Crimea during the war to see it, Aunt Selkirk went with her son in his yacht *Coral Queen*. She was taken up on horseback to the heights of Balaclava by a relative, Adrian Hope, to visit her old friend Lord Raglan, where they drove about together. She saw the cannons of Sebastopol firing but could not hear the sound of them.

Lady Katherine and I were great friends and companions, being both fond of riding and drawing animals. Once when staying with them her sister, Lady Isabella, said how ignorant I was and thought to improve my education, so set me a task to read so much of a history of the Reformation, and then be questioned about it. I thought it very dull and fell asleep with it open and could give no account of it when she questioned me. I liked Turner's *History of the Anglo-Saxons* and read it voluntarily; but I liked riding much better and to be out in the open air and drawing animals, in which I was encouraged. Lady Katherine and I used to ride to the farm houses and draw cattle. I sometimes sat close to their heads and drew them in strong perspective, the head large enough to hide most of the body and only show the hip bones. It taught me the shape of the animals, I learned all their shapes and had as it were a model of them in my head so that I could draw them as easily in one position as in another from recollection. I drew a great deal in that way and could do a portrait of any horse I looked at in three minutes, recognisable to its owner or groom. It surprised them but it was quite easy to me. I used also to do the likeness of the horse I rode as I saw it from the saddle with my knee in the foreground.

There was a noted pirate who haunted the southern coast of Scotland; he called himself Paul Jones although his real name was John Paul, a common name about Kirkcudbright where the name Jones is unknown. He came to the Isle intending to kidnap Lord Selkirk, but he was absent; so he carried off the silver plate or as much of it as he could find, the servants having hidden away the greater part of it. He took the silver tea pot used at breakfast time, and when he returned all he had taken, we found the tea pot to be still full of their tea leaves. All in all they were quite civil.

One of my friends was Charles Mackenzie,[17] brother of my brother-in-law James. I knew him well since he was twelve years old, he being a little younger than I. He was the most Christian man I ever knew. He went to Cambridge where he had great success as a mathematician. While he was at the University he heard a sermon preached by Bishop Selwyn pleading for young men to go as missionaries to South Africa. He immediately volunteered for that service. We were sorry that he gave up his brilliant career and what he called his 'artificial value' at Cambridge. He went to Natal and took two of his sisters with him, Anne and Alice. The elder, Anne, was sickly and he thought the change in climate might do her good. It was a Christian act as she was rather peevish and difficult to get on with, though pious and good, and much attached to him. Alice was very pleasant and a great friend of mine; we used to learn Milton together, she by sentences, I by lines. We used to be able to repeat great screeds of *Paradise Lost*. I taught her to ride as she would have to do so when in Natal. Charles

17. Charles F. Mackenzie (1825–62) accompanied John W. Colenso to Natal as his archdeacon (1855). Bishop of Central Africa 1861.

had several churches and had to ride as the distances were too great to walk. He had never been accustomed to riding, and the animal he bought was an unmanageable beast and threw him off each time he mounted it. He was very gentle with it, and when he fell off he just got on again till the animal got tired of its pranks and carried him quietly. At first his position did not seem satisfactory as the colony was disturbed by high and low church disputes which he worked to pacify, and doubtless did good.

11.5 × 9.25 cm. Watercolour, 1857.
Hugh with Margaret and William
fishing for mackerel in Loch Ailort.

WHEN I WAS NEARLY seventeen I went to London for the first time and spent some months with my cousins the Colviles in their house in Curzon Street. It was our custom when one of us was going away for the family to have an oyster supper on the previous evening; on this occasion Charles Mackenzie joined us.

There was no railway then. We went by sea in very good steamboats from Granton to Blackwell. The steamers were supposed to make the voyage in thirty six hours but my voyages always lasted for forty eight. There was always a good deal of rough sea from the Bass to the mouth of the Thames.

I went alone and was supposed to be under the charge of a lady friend, but my time was spent with old Admiral Milne,[18] a friend of Aunt Selkirks. We walked up and down the deck while he told me sea stories. Another friend was a Colonel of the Inniskilling Dragoons who some years afterwards suffered shipwreck, and his wife became a nurse in the Crimea; he shared his tea with me. It was very good. The banks of the Thames interested me but I did not see any criminals hung in chains as I had expected to do. The country seemed very foreign to me, the tall trees were stripped to make faggots and looked to me like palm trees. When we arrived at Blackwall the Admiral took a hackney coach (there were no cabs then) and we drove through ten miles of crowded streets, the huge dray horses almost putting their heads into our coach window. When we arrived at Pall Mall I supposed we would stop at a house like the Reform Club; but no, we went on and on and at last stopped opposite a nobleman's house which had trees with crows' nests in front of it. It all looked rather shabby as if it might have been the Leith Walk in Edinburgh; but it really was a fine mansion with two stairs and a lot of drawing rooms, and twice as big as any house in Edinburgh. A rush of young cousins came downstairs to greet me. I took leave of my dear old Admiral and never saw him again.

Next day I was taken out to walk in Piccadilly but found it difficult to admire London as I have done since. I missed the stone houses in Edinburgh and did not at first even see the beauty of the Green Park, and only cared for the fine cart horses. The cab horses seemed a wretched lot, but the hansoms were attractive and new to me. Respectable ladies did not drive in them then, but one might with the governess or a male cousin. The buses too were new to me, but we did not go on them. The horses were very poor and were subjects for caricature by Cruikshank and the artists who preceded *Punch*. They were very ill used, not like the fine well fed animals such as one sees now. (The bus and tram horses now mostly come from France and some from Canada. They are as well kept and fed as possible and treated with consideration, having more than one rest day in the week.)

My cousins used to walk in the Hamilton Place gardens next to Apsley House. The great Duke of Wellington generally went out through the gardens. He was fond of children and had made acquaintance with my cousins and always shook hands and talked to them. I went with my cousins to the gardens and was introduced to the

18. Admiral Sir David Milne (1763–1845).

Above top. Detail
14 × 23 cm. Ink and watercolour.
13 April 1840. The Duke of Wellington
walking on Constitution Hill with
Jemima (in the checked dress) and her
Colvile cousins.

Above
9 × 13.5 cm. Watercolour.
Visiting Landseer.

Duke, and met him many times. He was short and with pronounced features, the chin being even more remarkable than the nose. He spoke abruptly and often said 'God bless my soul' if anything surprised him. One day we told him we had been to the country and had got two frogs and asked him what we should call them. He said, 'Call them Monsieur and Madame.' We did not have them long: one jumped into a basin of hot water and perished; we preserved it in a bottle of spirits—I forget what became of the other.

One Queen's birthday we went to the Horseguards to see the Trooping of the Colours. We stood near to where the Duke was with a lot of Generals round about him. He recognised us, nodded to us and spoke to us from the back of his chestnut charger—which delighted us much. I remember meeting him once on Constitution Hill when we were walking in a body. He took the two youngest Colviles by the hand and walked along with us while all the people we passed took off their hats to him. I dare say they wondered who we were. There were a lot of us; it was very funny and must have looked like a girls' school!

I had promised my mother that I would do sketches for her every day. The Duke was the subject for many, often drawn from recollection.

I was taken by Aunt Selkirk to Chantrey[19] the sculptor's studio. Some of my drawings were taken to show him. He did not care for the imaginary ones but asked for those from nature, which he approved of. I also got acquainted with Landseer, I think through James Colvile. He was asked to dinner and was very kind to me. He lent me some of his drawings to copy and gave me some little pencil drawings he had done when he was six years old. I was often in his studio in St John's Wood where he had a lot of dogs around him. I also went to Mulready's studio with Miss Newdigate; he had been her teacher and gave us both good advice. Aunt Selkirk got me some lessons from Frederick Taylor but I do not think I was much better for them. He was celebrated as a watercolour artist, but his drawing was not accurate and his style rather sloppy.

My cousin James Colvile[20] was very kind to me in Curzon Street, and used to take me out. He was much older than I, more like an uncle. He took me sometimes to the old Miss Berrys; they had a small house in Curzon Street, and used to receive their friends in the evening. They came between their dinner parties and evening entertainments. One met remarkable people: Rajah Brooke of Borneo, Thackeray, Dickie Doyle and Jacob Manners (a writer on *The Times*); he was very tall, as was Thackeray. Dickie Doyle was very little and so was I, so we talked a good deal together. There were clever people too, Frederick Elliot and other London notables.

It was, I think, on my second visit to London that Thackeray called on me as he was going out on his black cob for a ride in the Park. He brought some of his drawings to show me before, as he said, 'the engraver cut the expression out of them'. They were nicely done and he put a little colour on them, which improved them as drawings but could not of course be reproduced in the woodcuts. My Aunt Colvile

19. Sir Francis L. Chantrey (1781–1842).

20. Sir James W. Colvile (1810–80), Advocate General for East India Company, 1845 Chief Justice for Calcutta 1855. Succeeded to Craigflower on the death of his father, 1856.

12ʰ August
1862

17.8 × 25 cm. Watercolour. 12 August
1862. A shooting party comprising, left
to right: Jemima, Isabella Blackburn,
Capt. Robertson of Kinlochmoidart,
Andrew Blackburn, John McIsaac.

Detail
12.5 × 12.5 cm. Ink and Watercolour.
3 April 1840. The first of three sketches
Jemima made at one of Samuel Rogers'
celebrated breakfasts in 22 St James
Place, London. On this occasion she was
introduced to the Scots painter Sir
David Wilkie (1785–1841) who was
renowned for his fastidious and brilliant
studies of Scottish Lowland life.

did not approve of the friendship and discouraged his visits, so I had
to get out of it somehow; but I was sorry. She had heard gossip that
Jane Eyre, just published, was the history of Thackeray and his
governess. She returned from one of her visits and found that a copy
of *Jane Eyre* had come among the books from the library, and one
of the young ones was reading it with great interest. She immediately
sent it away. Some years afterwards I was with a pious friend who
told me what a fine work it was. I had made no attempt to read it
at the time, because when a book is supposed to be doubtful I preferred to be able to say that I had not read it. When I did, I found
it all my pious friend had said.

Sydney Smith used to dine sometimes at Curzon Street. He was
surprised to see me so small for, while in College in Edinburgh, he
said he had known 'thirty six yards of Wedderburns!' I went with
James Colvile to hear him preach in St Paul's. After church while
walking about in the nave he asked me if I had enjoyed his sermon.
I said he looked as if he were going to say a good thing. 'Did I not
say a good thing?' said he.

I went to the opera which was new to me. The hideous short puffy
petticoats, and attitudes with compass-like legs, all the weight being
supported on the nail of the great toe, made me shudder. I had an
idea that dancing might be beautiful as in prints of Pompei and as
it is now to be seen in London theatres.

When in London I had the luck to hear some of the finest singers.
Mario[21] had the most beautiful voice I ever heard; he was a little

21. Giovanni Mario (1810–83).

22. Luigi Lablache (1794–1858).

23. Grivlia Grisi (1811–69).

24. Marietta Alboni (1826–94).

past his best then. Lablache[22] was a magnificent bass, loud enough one would think to blow the roof off. Grise[23] was much admired but did not impress me. Alboni[24] had a lovely voice; Mrs Gartshore said it was like peaches. Mrs Gartshore had the voice I liked best of all. She was daughter of Sir Howard Douglas and about the most charming person I ever knew. She could sing anything and often gave us a musical sketch of an opera standing at the piano. The fine ladies in London called her Mrs Garcia and asked her to their parties to sing, but she did not like being shown off in that way. When we settled in Glasgow we looked forward to seeing her often, but alas she died about that time.

One of the amusements about this time was a breakfast with the poet Samuel Rogers, a queer looking little man. He had a pretty house and some fine pictures now in the National Gallery. There were various fashionable people at it. The only person I remember was Tom Moore. I had hoped to hear him sing some of his own beautiful songs but unfortunately he had a cold and was too hoarse—it was very disappointing.

Another sort of party I went to, which was called 'breakfast', would now be called afternoon tea. One I went to with Aunt Selkirk was at the Duke of Buccleuch's old Montague House. It was rather shabby compared with his house and garden now. Dean Milman, a handsome old man, was there, and walked about the garden with my Aunt. Both had been tall but were now so bent that they did not stand more than five feet high. There were delicious strawberries and iced cream to eat. I also went to Lady Shelley's at Putney; she was economical and did not aspire to strawberries. She had gooseberry fool!

While I was with the Colviles I met Mr Liston,[25] a famous surgeon, a tall man with very big hands. A new operation had come in to use, cutting a muscle in a distorted foot so that it might become straight, or in the eye to cure a squint. Jeanie Colvile had a squint and he operated on her with good effect. I had a frog at that time and he showed us the circulation in its foot. He was interested when I told him how I could keep them on earthworms. I have been lucky in having the acquaintance of surgeons. Sir George Macleod[26] used to be very kind in telling me how to tie up cuts, which was very useful here when we had no doctor within reach. I knew Lord Lister[27] well and often sat next to him at dinner parties in Glasgow. We talked in a low voice about the discoveries he was making. We had a long friendship and he was very kind to my nephew Captain Adam Blackburn[28] after his dreadful wound at Tel el Kebir, and to Jim Wedderburn[29] when he had broken his knee playing lawn tennis.

My Aunt Colvile had a great faculty of hearing; she always knew what everyone was saying at table although she was talking all the time herself. For encouragement she once told me I had conversed well—it rather disposed me to silence.

Jeanie[30] was the strong one of the Colvile family. She could walk far and fast and was most willing to do messages for anyone. She was subject to rheumatism later in life and felt the change dreadfully. I have seen the tears in her eyes when she had to ask me to pick

Detail
8 × 7.2 cm. 21 November 1843. Sydney Smith (1771–1845) probably painted when visiting the Colviles' house in Curzon Street, London.

25. Robert Liston (1794–1847), Professor of Clinical Surgery, University College London 1885. First to use general anaesthetic in a public operation on 21 December 1846.

26. Sir George Macleod (1828–92), senior surgeon at the civil hospital in Smyrna during the Crimean War. Regius Professor of Surgery, Glasgow University 1859.

27. Lord Joseph Lister (1827–92). One of the great innovative surgeons of the 19th century whose work in the introduction of antiseptics (1860) revolutionised surgery.

28. Adam G. Blackburn (1858–91), seventh son of Peter Blackburn. Lost his right leg above the knee at the battle of Tel-el-kebin. Was much admired for the way he coped with his disability and for never being heard to complain.

29. James A.C. Wedderburn (1849–) eldest son of Andrew Wedderburn.

30. Jean Colevile (1820–95), fifth of the twelve daughters of Andrew Wedderburn Colevile, died unmarried at Lustleigh, Devon.

up anything for her. She bore her martyrdom bravely; we could not but look upon her as a saint. Her eyesight was mercifully spared to her and she could read in old age without spectacles. She had a good memory and a great knowledge of history—and very accurate. I often referred to her and always got satisfactory answers. I was sorry she was so narrow, not in religion or charity but in church matters. She always made a face of disgust when I mentioned my dear and admirable Dean Stanley. It was not so with Dean Church; though almost opposite in church matters, the two Deans were always friends. They used to come to my afternoon teas in London arm in arm and look at my sketches, which interested them both for different reasons— Dean Stanley because they were true records of what I had seen, Dean Church from an artistic point of view. Dean Stanley was quite devoid of any appreciation of music.

Mrs Colvile's relations, the Edens, used to like to tease me about the Scotch; one of their sayings was that we all had red hair. One day a large party of us were at Astley's circus and I was much amused in looking round to see that all the red haired ones were either Edens of half Edens, and all the Scotch were brown, black or fair. I did a sketch in rememberance of it. Red hair was at that time thought ugly and a reproach—it has not been so since, so many heroines of romance are described as having red hair, or golden locks or such like. When I was young, girls despised fair hair and always liked to think their own darker than that of their companions. They also all wished to be tall, at least taller than their companions, and were disgusted when I told them a tall woman generally weighed ten stone or more. Young ladies certainly seem much taller than they used to be. I saw one once at the zoo who was said to be 6ft 4ins; she could look over the top of her guardian's hat. I do not think it is an improvement; besides, it dwarfs the men!

When I was in London Spurgeon[31] was becoming famous as a preacher. I don't know what his denomination was—I think Baptist— he preached on Sundays at a large opera house on the Surrey side near the Elephant and Castle. My brother Andrew happened to be in town and we went to hear him. Admission was by ticket only as there was such a crowd. We walked there one Sunday morning, several miles. The fashionable, distinguished people—of whom Ruskin was one—had boxes. There was no pulpit but a platform on which the preacher walked about, almost acted, sometimes suiting the action to the word. He had a fine powerful voice and could be heard all over the large house without apparently exerting himself very much. The subject of the sermon was the Sabbath. He emphasised, 'Six days shalt thou work; hear this, ye lazy ones.' It was fairly good but not equal to many of our Scotch preachers. In the afternoon we went out to Blackheath and went to church with some friends.

We caught it next day from our Anglican cousins for going to a dissenting place of worship, and from our Presbyterian ones for travelling on Sunday.

I think it was about 1846[32] that the Free Church began to quarrel with the Established about patronage, which they objected to, and

31. Charles H. Spurgeon (1834–92), Baptist pastor of Waterbeach 1852, moved to London 1854. Became so popular that Exeter Hall could not hold his audience. Ministered until his death at the Metropolitan Tabernacle which held 6,000 persons.

32. 1843.

wanted the congregation to choose their own preachers. After a meeting about it I saw a black train of ministers march out of St Andrew's Church, George Street, in Edinburgh. I was on the Calton Hill at the time. They gave up their livings which was noble of them though the cause was not worth it. I could not see the harm of patronage. They objected to the — — appointing his old family tutor. It seemed to me that he could not have been an unfit man as no gentleman would have had a tutor for his boys who was not an educated man of good character.

I used often to go to the British Museum. My escort was the Rev. M. Baker, brother-in-law to my Aunt, Lady Clerk. What I liked best to begin with was the Egyptian room and the mummies. Afterwards when I went with Sir Charles Newton[33] it was the Greek sculpture, of which he was a good critic. In later years Elizabeth Eastlake and I often visited the Print Room to see the Albert Dürer woodcuts.

In another visit to London I stayed in Park Street, Westminster, with my uncle Sir George Clerk. The Clerks were much into 'society'. One morning at breakfast Miss Clerk asked her brother about a party he had been to the night before. He said, 'It was very crowded and there was nobody there.' I was surprised at so contradictory a statement. There were frequent dinner parties then, mostly political. One time I found myself sitting next Lord Lincoln, afterwards the Duke

14.5 × 25.5 cm. Watercolour. A dancing class in Willis's Rooms. Jemima is sitting second from the left, her cousin Jean Colvile sixth from the left. Lord Shaftesbury, seen entering the room, was opposed to radicalism but still piloted successive Factory Acts through Parliament (1847–50). His coal mines Act of 1842 prohibited underground employment of women and of children under the age of thirteen.

33. Sir Charles T. Newton (1816–94), Professor of Archaeology, University College, London 1840. Keeper of Antiquities, British Museum, 1861.

of Newcastle; he was very agreeable. At another I sat next a very pleasant middle aged man, Mr Cornwallis. We got upon Milton and he was surprised at my knowledge and appreciation of *Samson Agonistes*.

While in Park Street the Duke of Wellington was going to give a ball at Apsley House. Sir George happened to call upon him and told him I was staying with him. The Duke wrote me an invitation card with his own hand (I have it still). I think I only danced once at the ball, with an old Scotch friend, Campbell Munro of the Grenadier Guards; I enjoyed it very much.

Among other parties I went to with the Clerks was one at Sir Robert Peel's when he was at the height of his fame. He had a fine collection of Dutch paintings which he showed me round himself after the guests were gone. They were very fine but I do not care much for Dutch pictures; they are beautifully done but of ugly subjects. My uncle and Sir Robert were great friends and used to discuss business on Sunday afternoons. I heard him speak sometimes in the House of Commons. He was easily recognised by his attitude, one hand on his hip and the other on the green table. We are much indebted to him for his improvement of the London police. Ladies can now walk about the streets by themselves. When I was first in London one had to be followed by a footman, generally a tall one with a long stick. I used to study my route on a map so that I might not have to ask him the way. Policemen got the name 'Bobbies' from Sir Robert. It was a matter of difficulty and danger in these times to cross the street, especially from the construction of one's bonnets which acted as blinkers. One could not see without turning one's head and it interfered also with one's hearing. There were none of those blessed refuges in the middle of crowded thoroughfares, as there are now, where the timid can stop and get the watchful bobby to help them across. Vehicles were not obliged to keep to their sides as they are now.

One day in Park Street Landseer called upon us accompanied by a very handsome fair young man. We thought it might be his nephew and continued to call him so. In reality it was the Hon. Frank Charteris, afterwards Lord Wemyss; Landseer had brought him to see my drawings.

34. Sir Richard Owen (1804–92), Curator in Museum of Royal College of Surgeons, Superintendent of the Natural History Department, British Museum 1856. A pre-Darwinian, he maintained a cautious attitude to evolutionist theories.

I became acquainted with Professor Owen,[34] afterwards Sir Richard. We went with him and his wife to see the Surgeons' Museums. He showed us the fossil bone of a large bird from New Zealand from which he conjectured the whole anatomy of the creature, and many other interesting specimens. He was a very tall man and wriggled when talking. We thought he resembled the picture of St Sebastian when full of arrows, and called him so. Mrs Owen was a lively little woman, very enthusiastic about the curiosities in the museum. Her father's occupation had been a preserver of specimens, in which she assisted. She took us into the chamber of horrors and showed us preservations of diverse diseases, growth of bones, and a picture of elephantiasis—a woman with a gigantic grey leg with her natural leg shown alongside of it, and looking as if she were proud of herself.

On my return to Edinburgh I was acquainted with a young student, Basset Tytler, who gave me some animal skulls and taught me how to clean and preserve them. I was afterwards able to add to his collection. Poor Tytler met with a sad death. He fell out of a boat while fishing in Loch Ness and after clinging to it for some time, drowned. It was a fearful grief for his mother whose only child he was. She was a widow, a sad gentle lady who might have sat for a picture of the Mater Dolorosa.

Some years later when I was staying with the Huttons at Putney Park I visited the Owens again in their villa in Richmond. The Huttons were very kind and used to ask people to dine when we were there; Galton and other interesting people. Mr Hutton, being a magistrate, took us to see the prison for criminals on the solitary and silent system. They were all well fed, only those in for a short time being fed on bread and water. They were not allowed to speak to each other and were kept several yards apart while out at exercise. They wore wide-awake hats coming down over their faces with holes for the eyes. In the chapel the seats were arranged so that they could see the clergyman but not one another, and were confined alone in separate cells, very clean but awfully dismal. It was a sad sight.

Two murders were carried out in London while I was there, one in Curzon Street. Lord William Burrell was killed by his foreign valet. He was found guilty and hanged. The other was a Guardsman shot by his lover in Birdcage Walk. He had ordered her to lead a degraded life to make money for him. My youngest cousin was at the schoolroom window in Park Street and saw it done. We were walking in St James's Park at the time and heard the shot; I remember wondering what it could be. The culprit excited much sympathy and was pardoned, which we were glad of.

The Queen's first visit to Edinburgh made a great sensation. She arrived at 8 a.m., far sooner than was expected. We went half way to Granton and saw her drive past. She drove about Edinburgh attended by the Scottish Archers. There was a reception held at Dalkeith Palace which we went to. It was a pretty sight in the Park to see the Inniskilling Dragoons galloping on the grass. My mother went to the reception and my elder sister and I were presented and kissed Her Majesty's hand. Just in front of us there was an old gentleman who often got his sword caught between his legs and ended by kissing his own hand instead of the Queen's.

What a dull place the world would be if there were not horses in it! Of all things I like riding best. My brother George was getting on with his ws business and was able to keep a horse, and a friend of his kept two at the same place, so I could ride any of them. My favourite was a huge animal, sixteen hands two, with good points but not beautiful to the indiscriminating eye. We called him 'Behemoth'. His paces were good and his trot easy. He was rather peculiar in his ways, sometimes standing up on his hind legs in the street, one could not tell why, unless he wanted to look in at the windows of the houses. He was a very good jumper and I used to jump him over the wooden things they set along the new part of the roads while they were being

Macadamised, and we often took a start across the fields and fences. He generally jumped willingly but sometimes refused, and what was worse, first refused and then turned when one did not expect him to. Once he refused for a long time to jump over a ditch, at last doing so on his hind legs like a kangaroo.

I have heard various discussions on the subject of cutting horses' tails. The grooms' theory is that the nourishment that goes into the tail is better employed in strengthening the hind legs. An otherwise intelligent man I sat next to at dinner said that the tail should not be amputated, as it balances the head and helped to keep the horse from falling over. This view surprised me. When I was in London I went to see the Queen's horses; she had scores of riding horses, the favourite being a flea bitten Arab. I saw the cream coloured state horses, also the black ones used by the Master of the Horse on state occasions. I have also seen some of the best brewers' horses, Barclay and Paulins', I think, but I do not admire them as much as Clydesdales which have better shoulders and step out better. I have read that draught horses should have upright shoulders that fit the collar better, so as to have the collar at right angles to the traces—surely it is better to have the horse well made and the collar shaped to fit it, then to have the horse to fit the collar. I have very seldom had an opportunity of hunting, though once took a horse, that had never been to a meet before, to a hunt at Hopetoun House. It was very excited and did not behave with much distinction. We galloped all day and saw the fox swim the canal but we did not attempt to follow him. We left off at Winchburgh, seventeen miles from Edinburgh.

Frederick Rogers,[35] a friend of James Colvile's, came to hunt at Craigflower. He was a very agreeable man and we took long drives about to show him the country. I often sat next to him and we discussed all kinds of things, foxhunting among others. He said that if foxes were not hunted they would not be allowed to live. I agreed, and thought the foxes would prefer a few years of jolly life to no life at all. He became engaged to Gingy Colvile and they were happily married. They took a little house in London. The cabmen did not know the Square as it had not been occupied long, so we used to direct them to 'The Grapes' public house. They all know the public houses!

Charlotte Yonge was a friend of the Rogers and was asked to stay while I was visiting them. It was a very small house and we were lodged in two little garrets next one another, and used to brush out our hair together before going to bed, and so soon became friends. She was very good looking with dark hair and fine eyes, spoke pleasantly and was a little above middle height. We talked of many things. I found her not at all formidable, as one feared she might be, being so well informed; one might almost say learned. We drove about London in Lady Katherine's carriage (which I used to call the gondola, it went so smoothly). I kept up the friendship as long as she lived, and got a good many letters from her while I was illustrating her books.

I often stayed with Frederick and Gingy. One day they had a dinner

35. Frederick Rogers, Baron Blackford (1811–89), Barrister. In sympathy with and (1845) contributor to Tractarian Movement. One of the founders of *The Guardian*.

party, mostly lawyers. I went down with Coleridge.[36] At dinner he began by abusing my brother-in-law the Judge (Colin Blackburn) as being the 'worst mannered man in England'; not altogether untrue but not a suitable dinner subject. We then discussed a bill before Parliament which interested me. It sought to stop the use of false weights and measures. I had heard that he opposed it as being against trade. I felt rather aggravated and said, 'What is the use of Government?' He answered in measured tones, 'The preservation of life and property.' I replied, how would that be better done than by giving proper food in *just* quantity? We were getting rather cross and my neighbour on the other side, Sir Samuel Bromley,[37] a good-natured and agreeable man, took up the cudgels on my behalf for which I was obliged to him. Eventually I decided to change the subject to fairy tales!

While in England I stayed some time in Greenwich Hospital with Charles and Lady Isabella Hope. They had apartments there, he being one of the Commissioners and also being in Parliament. The view from the windows obliquely across the square was beautiful, the barges and other traffic very picturesque. I enjoyed it very much. We used to take drives all around; the country was very pretty all about where the Crystal Palace now stands. I was always interested by seeing the pensioners assembling after call of fife and drum to go the church. There were very few legs among them in proportion to their arms. One naval officer had lost both his legs and it was most curious to see how cleverly he came downstairs like a compass on wooden legs, both legs having been amputated above the knee and the false ones of course being jointless. False legs nowadays are different and have joints to them like real ones. Lady Katherine and I used to visit the pensioners in their neat little cabins. They were as a rule not very contented.

I got acquainted with the Newdigate[38] family who lived in Blackheath. Miss Newdigate was near my own age and had many brothers. They were very musical people and had lots of dances. I exhibited to them Scotch reel steps, mounted on the sideboard in the dining room. They seemed to think them rather strange though I did them as neatly as I could. Reel dancing was not so well known to the English as it is now. Miss Newdigate later married an excellent man, Captain (later Sir) Lynedoch Gardiner. He served in the army until he was superannuated and afterwards did many good and charitable works in the slums of London, especially among crippled boys. He set up a hospital for those between the ages of eight and fourteen. There already existed hospitals for them before and after, but between these ages they were apt to take to begging, having no other means of subsistence. Sir Lynedoch Gardiner is now dead but his hospital goes on and is a beautifully kept place on Blackheath.

When I went to Leamington in Warwickshire with my mother and sister we met Miss Newdigate, her father having some property near by. She took me visiting to fine country houses; I saw archery meetings frequented by the great ones and we danced till dark on the turf (not reels however!). While making myself fine for the archery meet-

36. John D. Coleridge, first Baron Coleridge (1821–94), Solicitor General 1868, Lord Chief Justice of England 1880.

38. Charles Newdigate (1816–87), MP for North Warwickshire 1843–85.

11.3 × 16.2 cm. An illustration from *The White Cat* published by Blackwood and Sons (1848). Jemima drew and lithographed the plates herself.

ing I bought a pair of gloves in Leamington, the worst I have ever had, mis-shapen things with the thumbs only half the usual length. My sister and I used to take long walks out into the country, once so far that we took the railway home from Coventry. The country and especially the trees are very fine in Warwickshire, especialy on the way to Shakespeare's house where there were the biggest elms I ever saw. At first I missed my native hills and the blue distance, one only saw so many rich grass fields and big trees. Afterwards on the way home I thought big hills rather clumsy things. Such rivers as we saw in Warwickshire were like stagnant ditches, and spread mist over the fields when the sun went down. Frost came early and killed the dahlias long before it did so in Scotland. The purpose of our going was for my mother's health, to see a celebrated doctor there. He was a rough spoken man and had cured many people. He did her no good; but afterwards she got better under the care of Dr James Simpson, the celebrated inventor of chloroform. I don't think people need go out of Scotland to look for better doctors than they can get in their own country.

When in Leamington I took something they called swinepox (I had never been near pigs). An apothecary was called in. He said I was 'going straight on' and I would 'soon come round and be all square again.' So I did, but bear a few marks of it even yet. I made a coloured drawing while there, of Pharoh in the Red Sea, I gave it to Lady Selkirk; it was to become the first of my Bible Beasts. My first publications were done by Blackwood in Edinburgh, the fairy tales of *The White Cat* and *Fortunio*—they were soon sold off.

About this time Landseer presented the Royal children with some fairy tale drawings of mine for which I got thanks through Miss Skerret, the Queen's private secretary. I got leave to draw the Queen's dogs at Windsor. My Aunt Mrs Colvile went with me. We wished very much that the Queen might be seen walking about but she did not appear. I did a good many drawings of the dogs and gave the Queen one of a fine Scottish deer hound which was accepted and I was thanked for.

I was in London on 10 April 1848, the day of the great Chartist meeting. The streets were empty; all the young men were employed as volunteers to keep the streets. They had batons, and we have one still hung up in our lobby as a trophy. My oldest brother kept guard in Jermyn Street with Louis Napoleon. My cousins came in now and then and reported all was quiet. We did not get out except for a walk in St James's Park. The Duke of Wellington made all the arrangements. The public offices were provisioned and all went off quietly. At the time I thought it the dullest day I had ever spent in London, but have since looked back upon it with great interest.

I should not like to renew my youth or even be younger than twenty five or thirty. I should like to remain at that age. It was jolly and one was strong and not afraid of anything or anybody.

After the Queen's visit to Edinburgh a party of six of us went on a Highland tour. Our leader was my sister, Mrs James Mackenzie, as her husband had connections there. The others were the Blackburn brothers, Colin, Andrew and Hugh. We started by the Inverness coach; Hugh and I were on top. We got to Inverness at one the next morning. We breakfasted on every possible luxury, though the nicest thing we got to eat in the Highlands was oatcake and bramble jam. On passing a beautiful river, we saw two picturesque figures in Highland costume standing on the rocks—the Sobieskies—who claimed to be descendants of—Prince Charlie.

We had three wet days in Skye and tried to get to the Storr rocks. We ladies turned back as it was so wet, but the gentlemen persevered and got to them and got back to the inn at Portree rather late.

We returned passing Kinlochailort on the way, and on looking down towards the sea thought that there must be a beautiful place around the corner. We found out in later years that there was indeed when Hugh and I bought Roshven.

A great part of the land journey was done on foot as carriages were not in vogue and travelling was then difficult. The scenery was fine. We came back via Loch Lomond, driving by the road as there was no steam boat then, and called at Killearn. It was very enjoyable on the whole.

HUGH BLACKBURN and I were married in St John's Episcopal Chapel, Edinburgh, by Dean Ramsay on 12 June 1849. Hugh had recently been elected Professor of Mathematics in Glasgow College. He had only one formidable rival for the post, Mr Stokes,[39] but he gave up as he would not take the tests. We started our honeymoon at Dalquhourn, then rented by Hugh's mother. Then we went on a walking tour of Switzerland. Before leaving London we invested in some Turkish carpets for our college rooms; they lasted well and are still in use today. We did not get many marriage presents, but those we did receive were handsome. It was the custom then for only

39. Sir George G. Stokes (1819–1903), Mathematician and physicist. First to use spectroscopy as a means of determining the chemical composition of stars.

near relations to give marriage presents. I only got four from acquaintances, quite unexpectedly. It was not the fashion to advertise marriages beforehand as it is now.

Before reaching Switzerland we visited Paris where we got delicious things to eat at 'The Kings' restaurant, saw plays and a very good circus. We watched beautiful trapeze performances by Léotard, a very well built man but with an ugly face and receding forehead. Leighton introduces this figure in a fresco of his at Kensington in the same position and exactly like a photograph I have of him.

We were good walkers in those times and could do sixteen miles a day. We did not do any of the wonderful feats our young people perform now on the Matterhorn—only ordinary long walks. We had a very good guide for the glaciers, Victor Tairraz, who had been with Professor James Forbes when he was studying the motions of the glaciers. I much enjoyed walking on the mountains and glaciers; it was like a new world, as if we had gone to the moon. One of the things we saw in Switzerland was the St Bernard's. I was disappointed in the dogs which looked like mangy collies. The monks' dresses were most unpicturesque and the monastery was more like a second-rate spinning mill. I should have liked to go to Mont Blanc but it was too expensive.

The place we liked best was the Faulhorn. We preferred going to it rather than the Mighe which was frequented by tourists. The first time we went I rode up on a horse. There was a wretched little inn at the top. They gave us what they called chamois for dinner, but I suspect it was a sheep I saw being killed when we arrived. They were going to wake us at sunrise but forgot; however the light woke us shining through the little ice coated windows. We dressed hastily and ran out. The scene was magnificent. There was an old German in a blanket who went into raptures over it. '*Wunderschön*', he exclaimed, '*klar geschnitt auf des Himmels blaue*', and so on. We were so impressed that we returned the following week on foot, up the other side of the mountain. A very hard walk especially as there was no good drinking water on the way. I drew a clutch of primroses though it seemed an absurd subject with such impressive landscape all around. There was at that moment a sea of clouds beneath us, the snowy mountains standing '*klargeschnitt*' above, and gaps in the cloud, so that we could see through to the green valley below.

The diligence driving in Switzerland was rather amusing (if driving it could be called). The driver tied the reins in a bunch to the splash board, cracked his whip, which he did loudly and skilfully, and repeated '*Nom d'un chien*' or such like expletives incessantly. We kept to the crown of the causeway and the other traffic had to avoid us or be knocked over. We occupied the *banquette*, a deep place on the top, under a hood, among the baggage.

After we settled in Glasgow we had visits from Professor James Forbes who had heard that I had been sketching from nature on the Swiss glaciers. He came to see my sketches and was much interested in them. At that time I do not think any one had done them from nature on the spot. Long after I saw some very fine paintings of them and the snowy mountains, in oils, done from nature. Now all the scenery has been so beautifully photographed it is well known to everybody. My sketches seem rather rough and commonplace; I had to do them rather quickly. I remember one day while I was in the middle of a glacier sketching a great rat running past me. This contrasted with the lots of pretty little butterflies that were flying over the ice. There were small bright flowers beginning to grow quite near the edge of the ice, especially at a well know spot called the *jardin* easily reached by tourists. I sketched some of the flowers there also.

We went to Switzerland again in after years. I rode all the land walks but of course had to walk on the glaciers. They were a good deal changed and the beautiful blue ice caves had vanished. We had poor weather and walked with waterproofs and umbrellas and sat on cold stones to eat our little luncheon with our feet in ice cold water—it no longer held any attraction for me.

When we returned from our Swiss tour we spent a month at Drumshang in Ayrshire so that Hugh might have quiet in which to prepare his lectures. I did not know anyone in Glasgow at first except for Professor and Mrs Ramsey[40] and William Thomson who was our greatest friend. He was like a brother to us. He and Hugh had met each other at Cambridge and had studied mathematics together in Paris.

In William Thomson's bachelor days an old aunt lived with him. One of her first pieces of advice to me was never to open the windows as so much soot and dust came in. I could not follow this advice. William was an enthusiast in ventilation and had many contrivances for it, open windows with gauze to keep out the dirt and heated plates to warm the air. He continued and improved upon this in his second house. I was asked to go to balls to chaperone him. The ballroom was a dirty trades hall badly lighted and with second rate music. William always used to ask me to take him home at 12 o'clock, but he was generally unwilling to come so soon! Another of our party was a Captain Charles Mansfied, a friend from Hugh's Cambridge days. He was a good looking young man and a good dancer. He used to write to me from the battlefields of the Crimea where he was secretary to Lord Clyde. Professor Rankine[41] also joined us sometimes, a very clever man and fond of dancing the lancers. He carried in his pocket a diagram of the rather complicated figures of that dance to keep him right.

Eventually the Glasgow people began to call on us and some country families also. When we began to dine out in Glasgow I was taken in to dinner first, being a bride, and put next to the master of the house, generally aged seventy: I resolved that when I gave dinners I should always endeavour to have some young people at them. An awkward thing happened before my first dinner party; my cook disappeared in the morning. We enquired at the railway station but she had not been seen, nor did the police know anything of her. What was I to do? I went to Mrs Ramsey and she lent me her cook who found all the preparations had been rightly made. The dinner went off well but I was very uneasy thinking that my poor cook might be

Detail
Photographic portrait of Lord Kelvin taken by Hugh Blackburn, 1 April 1856.

40. William Ramsay (1806–65), Professor of Humanity, Glasgow University.

41. William J. M. Rankine (1820–72), Professor of Engineering, Glasgow University.

at the bottom of the canal. Some days after I heard that she had got back to her friends in Edinburgh, having walked the forty two miles in her bed gown and slippers. She was a very nervous person and had taken fright that our dinner party might not come up to expectations.

Our dining room was very small; twelve people got in with difficulty and there was just room for the waiter to get round. The janitor, Macpherson,[42] waited, and did it well. He was a man of some importance; he had been a gentleman's butler, and excellent servant and a favourite of all. He used to carry the mace on high occasions and talked of 'me and the other professors!' He gave up waiting when his eldest son became a minister for fear he should have to stand him at dinner; besides he had made enough money. We had many interesting dinner parties. I have a record of one on Friday 6th February 1852 at half past six. Guests: Mr Sellars, Mrs C. Buchanan, Rudolph Schwabe, Mrs A. Buchanan, W. C. Buchanan, Mr Lushington, Miss C. Buchanan, Mr Dalziel, Mr A. Buchanan, Mrs Dalziel. Menu: Oyster soup, fried soles, boiled boned turkey stuffed with tongue, caper sauce, lobster quenelles, sweetbreads, leg of mutton. 2nd Course; celery, soufflé pudding, jelly, cranberries, ice pudding, wild duck, Stilton cheese. Dessert; cashew nuts, dried strawberries, figs, oranges, tamarinds, black currant cheese, thin biscuits. Wines: port, sherry, moselle, claret, curaçoa, brandy. Topics of conversation; Shakespeare, Scott, clairvoyance. I always took care never to have my menu the same. Conversation was always very varied.

Society was divided into different circles. One kept always meeting the same people and very often sitting next to the same person at company dinners, which was monotonous. Merchants were considered of a higher grade than manufacturers, which surprised me. I thought it was grander to make things than to make a fortune selling them.

Hansom cabs began to be used in Glasgow and I used to drive in them to pay country visits. Campbell's shop was instituted about this time and became famous; it was the first that had all sorts of things under one roof, from gloves to furniture. James Campbell was knighted when the Loch Katrine water was brought into Glasgow; he was Lord Provost at the time and a very wise old man.

Bill was born in the College on 23 March 1850. We had difficulty in naming him. The numerous Killearn branch of the family had absorbed all the family names so we went back to an old one; as the use of names is to distinguish one person from another we thought it best to give him one to himself. When I was sufficiently recovered we went to Edinburgh and he was christened by my old friend Dean Ramsay in St John's Chapel. His godfather William Thomson was not able to be present.

We rented a house in Ayrshire, Ardmillan. It was cheap, but damp and ill-constructed. It was built on a steep bit of rising ground with a court-yard and a small entrance. A tough ascent for coal carts; we used to get a ship load at a time. The carts had to be upset at the narrow gate, the coal then wheeled in to an enclosure and then carried

16.5 × 21 cm. Watercolour. 23 November 1850. Jemima and William in the rooms at Glasgow College.

11.5 × 11 cm. Watercolour. 1 December 1850. Hugh and Jemima feeding William.

15.5 × 22.5 cm. Watercolour. August
1862. The Blackburn children and
friends building sandcastles on the
beach in front of Roshven House.

into the house, wet or dry. The firelighting sticks we kept in the bath as it was of no other use. It was instructive to live there previous to our building our house at Roshven.

We had some very Sabbatarian neighbours near us in the College. They never went out on a Sunday except to walk to church, and kept their window blinds drawn all day. It did not seem to them that 'Let there be light' was the first commandment. A young lady of that family, Miss Reid, had been jilted by a young man of better birth who had been boarded with her father for the College classes. His family did not approve of the engagement so it was broken off. As she was in low spirits I thought it would do her good to get out of town and suggested that she came to Ardmillan with me. (I used to go down in April before the College broke up, taking the children with me.) She consented, and I started to become anxious as to how we should get through the Sunday. I knew I was sure of a good walk as the parish church was three miles off. I had to send the servants in the garden cart. Our nurse at that time, a good careful tidy body, did not approve of this, telling me of a pious family she had been with who never took their own horses out on the Sabbath, but sent for the postman's and a phaeton for their servants. After returning from church I persuaded my young lady that as it was a fine day we should sit in the garden. She was not willing at first but at length consented. She took out a sermon book and taught me some psalm tunes, without the aid of a piano of course—that would have been very objectionable!

Sunday noise was not allowed in Glasgow. One of our Professor's assistants had a piano which he played on Sundays, but the neighbours objected and got the police to stop him. It was not so in Edinburgh. Sunday was a dull day in Glasgow. The Forbes Mackenzie act, shutting the public houses on that day, had just been passed, and the streets were full of late-rising people lounging about.

A friend lent us seats in the Barony Church to hear the great Norman Macleod preach, and we used to go often. Dr Jackson[43] asked us to dinner to meet him and we became great friends for the rest of his life, and with his widow and family afterwards. I remember sitting next to him at dinner and discovering we were both inclined to look favourably on Pontius Pilate, whose worst fault he considered was being a place hunter, like many others who were not so much blamed for it.

Norman Macleod set up a sort of Ragged Church in the slums where workmen might go in their every day clothes and women in the 'mutches'. Many of the upper classes used to wish to attend it but he discouraged them. This church was far from his home so I asked him to dine with us, saying that I would not give any extra work about the dinner. He said, 'Oh, give me the best dinner you can.' This was the first I knew of his unsabbatarianism, though he had often amused us with stories of the distinctions they made, for instance using a knife to cut down meat for dinner but not using a saw. Some foolish and ignorant people accused Norman of wishing to abolish all ten commandments because he modified the strictures

43. Thomas T. Jackson, Professor of Ecclesiastical History, Glasgow University.

13 × 12.5 cm. Watercolour. May 1850. Hugh and Jemima looking towards Ailsa Craig from a hillside above Ardmillan House.

of the Sabbath. There was great horror expressed by some of the old ladies that sat in the Barony because the Precentor, who was a public singer, wore moustaches. They attacked Norman about it to make the man shave; but he would not do so, saying that as he had to go out at night they were a protection against the cold! This particular Precentor was a good singer, as were his family, and they helped greatly; sitting in different parts of the church encouraged the congregation to sing in parts. The singing was not always good. I remember Norman on one occasion getting up before the psalm was quite finished and telling everyone that it seemed they thought it religious to sing badly! The Macleods have a good ear for music so it must have irritated him very much. Norman Macleod was certainly a great preacher, not exactly eloquent, for when he was excited his words came out so fast it made him splutter. At the time of the prize fight between Sayers[44] and the American Heenan, his sermon was all about it with a text from St Paul. When we went out, a young officer who was with us remarked he had 'never been sorry before when a sermon came to an end'.

I had a large bulldog given me by my brother James. She had a white shaped head with a short crooked tail and was called Doll. She was not very clever but very affectionate, and was the terror of tramps when I took her out walking with me at Ardmillan. If I sat down she watched me and growled if any man came near. One day a man came running to tell me that a blast was going off, and she was fierce. After dark she would let women and children approach the house

44. Tom Sayers (1826–65), Pugilist. Was beaten only once during his career. His last and most famous fight with Heenan ended in a draw after two hours and six minutes.

Detail
11 × 16 cm. Watercolour. 16 October
1858. The death of Doll.

13 × 9 cm. Watercolour. 21 October
1858. The burial of Doll.

12 × 15.5 cm. Watercolour. The mathematician Archibald Smith hailing a boat from his yacht *The Raven* on the evening of 20 September 1850. Left to right: Archibald Smith, Jemima, . . .?, Hugh, William Thomson.

but not men. I remember during the Ayrshire election in which Hunter Blair and Mr Cardwell were candidates, a party coming to ask if we could put up their horse and trap, and I having to get up and hold Doll before they could get into the stable yard.

One year when we were at Ardmillan we had a visit from Archibald Smith and a friend of William Thomson's. They came in a little yacht called the *Raven*. A. Smith[45] was a son of Mr Smith of Jordanhill, who wrote an interesting account of a yachting cruise in the Mediterranean to prove that Malta was the island St Paul was wrecked upon. The friend was, I believe, a very clever and agreeable man; but the only thing I can remember about him was that he had a big hole in his stocking that I could not keep my eyes off. They embarked at night and we walked down with them to the shore to see them off.

45. Archibald Smith (1813–72), Mathematician and barrister, wrote on the deviation of the compass.

Lord Selkirk also visited us in his yacht the *Coral Queen*. He took us out to sail and we took Bill with us, who wished to carry his little coach whip with him to make the yacht go faster. It had little effect. We were becalmed and had to go ashore earlier than planned and send for our carriage, which we had sent to a village some ten miles away to await our arrival. We did not get home 'till ten o'clock.

Captain Mansfield also visited us at Ardmillan sometimes. He was wounded in the Crimea, and afterwards, being unable to go to India during the mutiny, went into diplomacy.

Almost all the drawings of my Bible beasts were done at Ardmillan. They were done out of my head without models, except the hand taking the dove into the Ark, and the hen and chickens, which were done entirely from nature. The legs of Lazarus were from recollection of a cripple I used to visit in my youth. In later years when I came to do *The Crows of Shakespeare* I once again worked without models, though a fall of snow helped me solve a problem I had with the black

Detail
17 × 24 cm. Watercolour. 28 July 1854.
Disembarking from the Earl of Selkirk's
yacht *The Coral Queen* after she had
become becalmed.

Detail
11.5 × 15 cm. 28 July 1851. Jemima and
Hugh observing an eclipse of the sun
from the front of Ardmillan House.

12 × 15.8 cm. Watercolour. Landing on the beach of Ardmillan on the evening of 5 August 1851.

on white of Romeo and Juliet. I remember going out and throwing snow on the back of a hen to see how it lay! The eagles in the drawings for Coriolanus were done from a captive bird belonging to the Duke of Argyll. My *Birds from Moidart* were done entirely from nature, backgrounds and all. Mostly I worked from living birds which I let go after drawing them.

There were about ninety students in Hugh's class at the University, chiefly farmers' sons. We used to ask a few of them to dinner sometimes. They all got themselves up in white kid gloves and were very shy. My nephew Colin Mackenzie was living with us and he and Donald Macleod were sort of go-betweens. The students were puzzled as to when to go away, so when one got up and took leave they all followed like a flock of sheep. Before we left Glasgow the class increased to between three and four hundred. The students then did not take more than three classes each session. The fees were three guineas in cash plus a pound for University expenses, and a further pound deposited for the use of library books—this was returned afterwards. They mostly brought provisions from their homes, some potatoes, oatcakes, casks of butter, with eggs layer about; thus living costs all together were about twenty five pounds.

We were often invited out to Lord Belhaven's house at Wishaw where we were kindly entertained. The railway was convenient so that we could get back in time for the morning class. Lady Belhaven was a most agreeable lady and an old friend of my mother's. She used to get up early to see us off in the morning and gave me bunches of beautiful flowers freshly picked from her garden. On one occasion when I was going to Wishaw there was a most amiable looking old gentleman in the railway carriage with us in blue muftees—which I thought probably the gift of a grand-daughter. To my surprise when we got to Wishaw the Belhaven footman introduced him to me as the Duke of Richmond. We discovered that we had the same destination and got into the carriage together and had much pleasant talk. He told me that it was his mother who had given the ball on the eve of Waterloo at Brussels. We returned to Glasgow in like manner, and as he had no servants with him he was going to help me with my baggage. I thought him too old and frail even to manage his own green tartan carpet bag, and made haste and got a porter. Afterwards he asked Hugh to dinner at the Barracks (a wretched place then in Duke Street). The Yorkshire Militia of which he was the Colonel were stationed there while the regulars were in the Crimea. Hugh found him old fashioned in his talk.

Professors were held in greater esteem in Glasgow and Edinburgh then, and there was seldom any social gathering without some of them being invited. We did not know any of the Edinburgh professors except James Forbes, and we knew him as himself, not as a professor.

We dined frequently at Possil House with Sir Archibald[46] and Lady Alison. They were in high society which she, indeed both of them, had a turn for. We met with good company there. On one occasion after dinner I was sitting with a lady. In front of us on a table there was a dinner plate with a lot of visiting cards on it. I recognized some of the names and asked if they had been in Scotland recently. I was told that the cards had been left on Lady Alison in London. It seemed somewhat ostentatious to exhibit them; they were mostly of the nobility, the 'best people' as they are called by some. No doubt the Alisons moved in the highest circles of society but they were nevertheless kind to their poor relations. When I was staying at Possil with my mother we went to the Episcopal church in Glasgow on Sunday. Before the service ended Lady Alison's footman brought her in her letters, which to my surprise she read there. I was told after that Lady Peel was very ill and that Lady Alison was concerned to hear of her.

Their eldest son was a distinguished soldier, and when he returned from the Crimea and went to church at St Mary's 'The conquering hero' was struck up on the organ. At his marriage afterwards to the rich Miss Black, the church was so crowded I saw women trying to climb over the rails outside to get in. Even with the help of a policeman we, who had tickets, could hardly get in to witness the ceremony. Sir Archibald was very industrious and besides his heavy Sheriff work, to which he walked in from Possil every morning, he helped his sons with their studies when they were attending Glasgow College. He was very brave too. When Glasgow was in a very disturbed state from political rows he went in to a conspirators' den alone, up through a trap door. They were too much taken aback to hurt him. It was very dangerous but he was very military and would have made a fine soldier.

When Bill was old enough to be left in the charge of his nurse and Hugh's mother we went on a tour to Northern Italy. At Genoa we were joined by William Thomson and a friend whose name I forget; they preferred coming by sea. We were much fascinated by Mentone which was not then a resort for the English, and then spent

46. Sir Archibald Alison (1792–1867), Historian.

Detail
17.8 × 12.5 cm. Watercolour. 5 May 1874.
Pineta Ravenna.

three weeks in Florence where I did many drawings both of the scenery and of the old pictures. William frequented the University at Pisa as he had some acquaintances there (they had beautiful green frogs for experimenting on. When I admired them they gave me two which I should have liked to bring home with me. I did not think I could do it so let them go in the Arno). We wished to have our dinner at home in our lodgings, but we found that nasty, so we took our evening meals out at restaurants. We took a number of walks, I remember, in the Carrara marble quarries. Hugh found walking rather hot so he took a nap in the shadow of a rock.

We went on to Venice via Bologna. On the journey we met with Rudolph Schwabe who was very pleasant. He and I talked a great deal in the coupé of the coach while Hugh snored. We met again at Venice where I also met and went about with Mrs Denniston—she said something about Glasgow and Mrs Schwabe asked in astonishment if we came from Glasgow. We had been at art galleries together and talked after but, as is the custom with Scotch people, never told each other where we were from. Photography was just beginning and Hugh and I got done; mine was rather the worse as I was much bitten by mosquitos when at Padua.

We returned from Italy by the St Gothard. I did not like Switzerland after Italy. We travelled over the pass in a supplementary diligence, the big one being full. There were two Italians next to us who had the best seats, such as they were. They never offered to change and as there was little room we spent a very stuffy uncomfortable night. I angered one old man very much by opening the window at night.

When we got to London we went to the Great Exhibition in the

Crystal Palace in Hyde Park, which Prince Albert hoped would help bring peace to the nations. It was followed by the Crimean War and soon after by the Indian Mutiny.

I first met John Ruskin at the Alisons' house in Edinburgh and we became great friends. This was about the time his books were beginning to get him great fame. We used to enjoy going to exhibitions together, and after we had looked at a good many pictures he always took me to a restaurant and fed me on mulligatawny; then we would return to the exhibition to look at more paintings. When in London I used to visit him at Denmark Hill to see his pictures. His parents were still alive then. I remember breakfasting with him on Millais' twenty fourth birthday, when we had shrimps which Ruskin had to teach me how to manipulate. Millais was a most handsome young man whose paintings were just starting to get famous. Ruskin used to visit with us in Glasgow. On one occasion when the much admired Mrs Ruskin was with him we went to look at a fine church with a lovely spire built by Pugin. It was foggy weather so we returned quickly and sat each side of the fire and talked. He was first rate at 'twa handed crack', and was not at all formidable as one might have expected from his books. We asked him if there was anybody he would like us to ask to meet him at dinner. He suggested Alexander Smith[47] whose poems were making some sensation then. Norman Macleod also joined us and we had most pleasant entertainment. I wish I could remember all the epigrammatic things that were said. The party was, I think, ten in number: Mr Ruskin, Dr Jacobson, Mr A. Smith, Norman Macleod, Mr C. Taylor, Miss Davidson, Mrs Jacobson, Mrs Ruskin (who looked very pretty and bright). The conversation was very general, turning on poetry and painting. Alexander Smith came late. I remember him surprising me by asking if I ever walked on Glasgow Green by moonlight! On another occasion we invited Alan Mackenzie to meet Ruskin.

Ruskin's marriage with Mrs Ruskin, née Gray of Perth, was not a real one. She afterwards married Millais who also used to visit us in Glasgow. Some years after, we were friends and I used to visit them in their fine house in Kensington. One day when I called he was painting a figure of a girl and he asked me if I thought it rightly drawn. I made some criticisms and suggested an improvement in the folds of her black satin dress, which he immediately carried out.

I have known many artists. I knew Sir Daniel Macnee very well and he introduced me to others; to Peter Graham, the best of landscape painters, great also in Highland cattle, a very pleasant little man with a nice wife and children. I have dined with him and sat next to H. B. Davis, a very agreeable man whose works I admire very much. I went with Macnee to his studio, which was Landseer's in St John's Wood. I was often there before as I knew him well. I went also to MacWhirter's and we called at Alma Tadema's but did not find him at home.

My daughter Margaret was born at Ardmillan on 28 September 1852, and when Thackeray came to Glasgow to give his lectures on the four Georges she was still a small child. He came every night

47. Alexander Smith (1829–67), author of *Life Drama* (1851), *City Poems* (1857).

12 × 17.5 cm. *c*. August 1853. Hugh, Jemima and Doll walking by the sea near Ardmillan.

to the College to supper, either to our house or at William Thomson's—which was very pleasant. Lady was romping and tumbling about; I told her it was not 'Ladylike' to do so. Thackeray remonstrated; but I said it was better to stop it before she was old enough to remember it, and he agreed I was right.

After staying five years at Ardmillan we thought we would rather have a place of our own so we set off to look for one. We took a steamer to Campbeltown, then drove on to Tayinloan, and finding it a stinking little place walked on a further nineteen miles. I walked very comfortably but Hugh often stopped to drink water. We got to Tarbert and I felt much inclined for tea but found I could not swallow. That night I found myself burning hot and when I cast off the bed clothes I shivered. My neck was very red. We went on the following day by the canal boat on which there was a most diverting helmsman, but I was incapable of being amused. The following day was Sunday and I went to church. Hugh was not well enough to accompany me and stayed at home in the little inn on a horsehair sofa, open mouthed over a spittoon. In church I did not know if they were singing Gaelic or English, and the place seemed to be spinning round; so I went and sat for a while on the doorstep, and in time went home. That afternoon we went to the doctor's; he was away and his assistant looked into our throats and said we had caught colds and recommended a gargle, which we took. His fee was one shilling. When we arrived next day at Oban the only sustenance I had been able to take was a strawberry. We established ourselves in the best hotel, then walked to the doctor, who was a good one. He felt my pulse which was about 120 (a hot day and me in a greatcoat). He asked if I had had any redness. I said I had, and he pronounced it scarlatina. We asked what we were to do? He said, 'Remain where you are; all the people where you are staying had scarlet fever in the spring.' So we stayed. I went to bed and was so stiff for eight days I could not turn myself in bed without help. I then took many warm baths with disinfectants and drank herb teas. Eventually I grew stronger and we then went out walks and drives. When I felt quite well and strong we went to Skye where I frequented the solitudes of Loch Coruisk—then home.

When we went from home I usually asked the doctor to go out once a week to see if the children were all right. We had not done so this time so I wrote to him. He said there was no scarlet fever there. I suppose I got it at the stinking inn at Tarbert where the room had not been cleaned out. People were not so particular about infection then as they are now. I do not know what the fate of my greatcoat was; it was stolen. I had worn it day and night all the time I was ill but don't think it could have given the infection as it was before the time for it to be dangerous. When we got back to Ardmillan I had all my garments boiled, but not my sketch book album in which I had recorded all our adventures. Books are supposed to carry infection but I have never heard of anyone burning their Bibles and prayer books, though they burned everything else, even their carpets.

When we had settled to leave Ardmillan we had a sale of most of our furniture, except some chairs we thought worth keeping. Our strong Scotch carpets which had lain for three years were bought by a manufacturer to make waxcloth. A second hand writing table I had brought for thirty shillings went for more than that price. Some kind friends attended the sale and helped it on—everything went for more than we had paid for them except my two Guernsey cows. Though they had been much admired by the neighbouring farmers for the richness of their butter, they were sold well under their real value at eight pounds each; we had paid thirteen for each of them. It was a day of bad weather and they did not look their best, but we had had the good of them for five years so need not complain. We took with us some of the plants from the garden.

Before we left Ardmillan Barbara Macfee (Babs) engaged herself as a maid to us thinking we were to remain in Ayrshire, her native country. However she came with us when we did move. I had a very vicious cockatoo which I fed and attended to myself as it was very fond of me, tho' so ill tempered to every one else. Barbara did not like me to do so, and to save me trouble she took it in hand. One day it bit her badly but she only said, 'Poor beast, it did not mean it; the nurse had been teasing it'. The nurse was an unworthy person. I had to dismiss her summarily between terms and was at a loss to get another, so Barbara said that she could undertake the charge until next term when I would be able to find another. (It is rather difficult to get the best servants between terms as they usually, in Scotland, arrange themselves for six months.) She had been used to take care of her younger brothers and sisters, being the eldest of the family. When it came to be term time I began to look for a nurse, but she said she would like to remain nurse for another term which I was glad to hear, and so from term to term she remained with us for many years. She was a large woman, her bosom an ample couch for the children.

11 × 8.25 cm. Watercolour. August 1856. Barbara MacFee feeding a horse from one of the windows of old Roshven House. Left to right: William, Margaret, Barbara MacFee (Babs), young Hugh.

Overleaf
10.7 × 12.5 cm. Watercolour. September 1859. Jemima drawing a seal, drowned in fishermen's nets.

When they were all past nursing she developed a turn for cooking and was cook for many years, enslaving others to help and getting the ploughman to stir the jam and assist in any way they could. She was very industrious and unconventional. She could turn her hand to dairy or any other work, and would do up a shirt at the nursery fire, and 'spoiled the place' as her contemporaries said. Eventually she became our housekeeper and only left us when her health failed and she went to live with a younger married sister. She came from a respectable well off family in Ayr; she was not so well educated as her sister Sarah (who was also with us for several years), but could read and write a little. She knew many old songs and ballads which she would repeat, and spoke the purest of Scotch, which I liked, so the children were not exposed to the vulgar English as some of our neighbours' children were, whose parents wanted them to have an English accent. When Bill went to Eton straight from Scotland he was laughed at for his Scotch accent and expressions: he asked for a lexicon which he said he 'needed'; his companion said that was not right ... he should say he 'wanted' it. 'I don't want it; I need it', he replied. The Scotch use the word 'want' often—'I want something'; 'You may just want it, but I won't want it' (meaning to do without it). He also got out of the habit of pronouncing the letter R strongly and when he was learning Italian had some difficulty in recovering it.

Our servants as a rule stayed with us. I remember one saying to me, 'You don't know, Mam, what servants are; you only have us and we are at home, only more comfortable.' It is a divine blessing to have trusty and much attached servants.

IN 1855 WE BOUGHT a small property on the beautiful west coast of Inverness-shire. We chose a part that had no crofters on it, as we did not know much about Highlanders then and did not think they would be pleased to pay rent to strangers; still less would we like to force them to do so. There was a half rotten old house on the place, two stories high with dilapidated attics above. The passage to the kitchen had a roof that let in the rain, so on wet days we had to go on stepping stones to order the dinner, not an easy thing to do—even on dry land. Dinner was not to be easily got, for the sheep we had bought from the late proprietor at a high price, as was the custom of the country, were little better than skeletons. The fish depended on our own catching, and vegetables there were none. A neighbouring proprietor sent us his surperannuated gardener, a useful servant. He dug two yards in what had once been the garden and sowed it with peas. The garden was unenclosed save for an old wall on one side and was open to sheep, which I now and then had to drive out with my pet bulldog assisted by a collie. After our so-called gardener's efforts he felt his back tired and gave up the work. There were no fences on the place. A foal used to come into the house and take away our door-mat to play with and the cows spent the day in the shadow of the house.

It was the custom of the time for the sheep-owning proprietors to club together and keep a fox hunter among them, who was not the most reputable man in the country. He and his dogs located themselves upon us for a time each alternate month. He used to invade the kitchen at the most inconvenient times when our meals were being prepared and demand food for his dogs, a mangy pack consisting of a foxhound and six or eight small terriers. I put up with the nuisance in the hope of seeing a fox hunt. The man spent the day lying by a haystack half asleep in the sunshine. I asked him when the hunt was going to come off. He said there would not be one as there were no fox cairns on our ground. We have got rid of all that now and keep down the foxes by our own endeavours.

We soon found it necessary to do something towards improving the house, so we got an architect to come and see the place and make plans. We sent our boats to meet him at the steam boat. He did not like its look. He called it 'a four-oared paper boat'. The contract on the building was taken by a local man who installed his drunken brother to do the work. Sixteen masons arrived without provisions or any arrangement for their up-putting, and no quarry men. We had to locate the masons in a shed near the house and on the first day feed them on haggis prepared for our own dinner.

The house was begun crooked, not of the size nor of the hewn stone contracted for; so we had to get a clerk of works to look after matters. This added a good deal to the expense, otherwise not excessive, as the materials could come by sea. The clerk of works had it taken down and begun again rightly. The workmen as soon as they had earned some wages went off and drank them at the nearest public house. The wood contracted for was to be pitch pine. An inferior kind was sent all in hopes of us being so far off it might not be

21.5 × 25.5 cm. Watercolour. 1859.
Unloading materials for the rebuilding
of Roshven House.

returned—but it had to be. I asked the clerk what was each trades-
man's way of cheating? He said that plumbers sent light weight of
lead, plasterers hairless plaster, etc. He was a very intelligent man
and as there was no other place to put him, part of the old house
having to be taken down before the new was built, he had to lodge
with us. He gave us much information on the working classes. He
had been a stone mason and was a very good carver. He made us
a beautiful sundial out of some leavings of freestone. It was carved
with plants, birds and sea creatures from my drawings. When he was
afterwards employed building Fettes College in Edinburgh he used
some of the designs for decorations.

We found it necessary to put up some fences so got a man from
the Lowlands to come and do it. 'Wise John' as we called him had
been much employed in such work in such places, and he had to put
up where he could. He gave our servants much information about
lice, a prevalent plague in the country, which I have found useful
both here and when travelling in Egypt. I generally found myself
infested with them after visiting in crowded cottages.

The parish doctor at that time was much addicted to whisky, that
curse of the country. The first time I saw him was when I was out
fishing one evening. I saw a man riding up and down the path leaning
over as if he were looking for something he had dropped. I asked
my rower who he was. He answered, 'The doctor drunken.' All the
same the people liked him and thought him a good doctor. When
typhoid fever was raging in the country we had to employ him, and
while in the house with work to do he kept quite sober, but when
he left us he was found dead drunk in the road. In later life he left
off the evil habit and lectured on temperance to those who had been
tempted as he had been.

Our post used to come to a place eight miles off three times a week
and a boy had to go and get the letters, so if one wanted to answer
them by return one of us had to ride over with the letter. When the
parcel post began we sent for so many parcels that the one man then
allowed us by the Government could not carry them, so a second
had to go along with him, still three times a week. At last it was thought
fit to send one every day, and we now have a daily post, mounted
and in uniform. There will soon be a railroad within five miles which
will bring us into civilization.

When we first moved to Roshven there was no school so we brought
a young school mistress with us. She lived with our servants for the
summer months to teach our servants' children. Then we got a
schoolmaster when we had a cottage to put him in. He was an old
engineer who hopped about on crutches. He had no patience with
the incapable children but was very successful with the clever ones,
some of whom have got on really well in life. Now of course we have
a board school with an excellent teacher. To solve the religious difficulty I agreed with the priest as to what printed matter was to be
put up on the walls of the school room and for special religious teaching he took the children of his flock in to the chapel. Only a very
few children were of protestant parentage.

There are ghosts in this country who have been seen by some. Persons who have met with sudden death are supposed to walk. One haunts this house and is heard walking along the passage at night. He used to knock on my bedroom door but when I called 'Come in', he never appeared. There are wonderful dreamers. Once a child was lost and a woman dreamed where it was to be found, and they found it where she had said, dead. It had followed the peat cutters up the hill unnoticed and had died in a bog. A sailor was drowned and was not found for weeks. A woman dreamed, and he was found sitting on the shore with his head covered in snow when the men went to cut sea-weed. Another ghost has the form of a dog which runs about at night with a broken chain rattling after it.

There was not much society or other distractions at Roshven and that is when I took to studying the fauna and writing about them.

Our second son Hugh was born in Glasgow on the seventh of February 1855. There was an awful storm the night before. The Old College in the High Street was a very sheltered place; one seldom felt the wind there but that night it roared continuously. Bits of the carved work fell in the street with a great clatter. We moved the bed in the nursery away from where the chimneys might fall. A can fell on a skylight and let the wind in. We got it shut with a struggle. Next morning the street was covered by broken cans and chimney stalks. Hugh was born at about eleven and did not breathe at first till he got a draught of air from an open door. Alice Mackenzie[48] who was with us then had an aquarium which she kept in the drawing room with a spoon beside it for lifting the sea beasts. A waggish neighbour who called one day, James Hope-Scott, asked if that was for feeding the baby to make him such a fine child. However when he got to Roshven he throve well, Babby took his cradle to the kitchen with her when she cooked the dinner and gave it a shove with her foot when her hands were full. The kitchen was also a refuge for sick lambs and poultry. He was much out of doors.

When he was a year old he teethed badly, for his teeth were slow of coming and then too many came at once and made him ill. One night in Glasgow when I was sitting up with him, I heard the fire drum beat and looking out saw the sky very red. It was Stewart and MacDonald's warehouse on fire. Next day I heard that a fireman had been killed and the newspaper said that there was no fund for the widows and children of firemen killed in duty, only an allowance for the injured till they were fit to work again. I thought I would like to do something for them, so painted an oil picture of an engine starting for a fire. I did it in the engine house and the men sat for me, and the horses. (The white one had been in the Scots Greys and was a spirited animal; when the fire drum was tapped it began to prance and make ready to start at the gallop. It was soon after sold and being put in a cart, fell down dead.) At that time a water cart went with the engines to start the water, and men took their horses out of their carts and the first at the spot got a reward, as also the first engine. I exhibited the picture at the Edinburgh picture exhibition but put too high a price on it, so it did not sell. I engraved it on stone and

48. Author of *The story of my Aquarium* or *A Year at the Seaside.*

sold the copies at 2/6 each. They sold well—I sold some of them to MacDowall, the great London fireman. The present captain of the Brigade, Patterson, got hold of a few some years afterwards and had them photographed. I gave the picture to the Brigade and it hangs in the recreation room in their new premises. It was exhibited last year at the Great Exhibition in Glasgow. For some years afterwards the fireman had to drink my health at their New Year's supper. They sent me photographs of the taking down of the Old College Museum with their portraits in it. When I went to see their new place lately there was only one member of the Brigade remaining from those I had met previously, but I found I was not forgotten.

There are no fire escapes in Glasgow as they have in London as the stairs are all of stone. I heard from the former Captain, Bryson,

Detail
8.5 × 12.8 cm. Watercolour. 19 June
1858. Margaret falling off a donkey.

that he had only one case of rescue. They always had ladders attached
to the engines. A shop was on fire and there was a wooden stair to
the house above. Captain Bryson went up himself and rescued a
woman—he was afraid that his men might not be too steady as it
was New Year time.

My sister Isabella was a most unselfish person. Like my mother
she was very strong and enjoyed walking against a cold east wind,
saying it was pleasant and bracing. She took a very bad cough one
winter but took no heed of it and was often to be found staying up
all night with a sickly sister in law when she was in more of care
herself. It got so bad that she at last saw a doctor who found it a
bad case, and said she must go to a warm climate in winter; so Madeira
was fixed upon. She took with her her three young girls and a maid;
my mother also went with them. They set sail in November and when
they had been gone some time and I was expecting to hear of their
arrival there, I got a letter from my mother dated Liverpool, as
follows:

Neptune Hotel, Liverpool, 19th November.
Dear Jemima, Here we are after a cruise of eighteen days in
tempestuous seas, one gale after another; thunder, lightning, and
hailstones. I am thankful Isabella bore the weather and all dis-
comforts well, suffered less from sea sickness than most of us,
her appetite improved and was equal for the cheese and other
delicacies out of the Captain's best. There was a decided change
for the better in her cough as we got into milder air about 800
miles from this; but the evening and night of the 21st we had
a fearful storm, the vessel (said to be in a strong labour) groaned
and shuddered as if all the timbers were giving way! On the
morning of the 22nd her bow was under water; and when strug-

removal of the contents of the Old College Museum — *26th March*

17.5 × 25.3 cm. 26 March 1870. Moving the contents of the Hunterian Museum, which was part of the University, from the High Street to Gilmorehill. Jemima is third from the left, sketching the scene.

gling to right herself the *St Vincent* shipped a sea which took off her bowsprit, topmast, topsails and rigging till these were sent floating in the waves. We were in the greatest danger. Immediately after we shipped another sea which nearly carried the Captain and man at the helm overboard. How they escaped no one knows as the bulwark gave way. The jolly boat lost her moorings and had her side stove in past all repairs; and the other boat with a hen coop, a sopha, and table fastened to the deck, the safe for cold meat etc. were all washed over board; the binnacle carried to another side of the ship; the kitchens upset; the poor cook under the stove with the boiling water from the coppers upon him, and was only saved by another wave following to cool things down. The first mate, our best hand, got dreadfully crushed at the same time by the falling of the kitchen though it saved him from a watery grave.

We were most fortunate in our fellow passenger Mr Cropper,

a student of the Free Kirk who had attended some of the medical classes and took upon himself the post of surgeon. He got the mate carried to the cabin and laid him in his own berth, like a good Samaritan. Isabella tore bandages off her dressing gown; he was very faint, but after washing his face with eau de cologne and getting some brandy he slept for two nights and two days, then wanted up on deck saying 'anything was better than being like a log'. The Captain was thankful to have his advice on deck.

On the morning of the 22nd we were told 'man could do no more', and our only chance was if our deck rudder held we might drift to some port. For two days our fate threatened to drive through the Bay of Biscay. The Captain and all hands seldom left the deck; Mr Cropper helped everywhere, the womenkind did their duty in remaining perfectly quiet, and indeed a degree of resignation came over us past human belief. Isabella's composure surprised us all, and thanks to the good sense of Bella the children never had any idea of danger. She asked me once, 'What could we do without sails?' I reminded her that 'there were none on the Ark', and she said she would 'keep that in mind'. In all our perils it disturbed me more to see Isabella sitting in wet clothes with no fire in the ship than to think we might all commit our bodies to the deep. The Thursday the wind changed and hopes were given that we might make Cork. From the fog for some days no observation could be taken. On the 27th we signalled a large ship, the *Ant* of Glasgow. We said Bim (that's me) [i.e. Jemima] had come to help us. This gave us the longitude and latitude, and we found we could enter the channel. I said to the Captain when we saw the first high land on the coast of Ireland, 'Now we are safe'. His answer was, 'When we have a pilot on board and a smoker tugging us I shall be the happiest one, but not till then.' When by the blessing of Heaven this took place the Captain resigned the charge to the pilot and asked the steward to shave him and help him to dress; he came on deck a changed man, but it was with hectic cheeks and a nervous voice. The necessity for exertion was gone and nature gave way under his fatigue. He had scarcely slept for sixteen nights and few seamen had ever seen such a fortnight. I hope he may receive his strength soon. We may be thankful we had such a Captain, so perfect in the management of his ship. His having come to port in her disabled state seems the astonishment of the seafaring people who boarded us on arrival.

We are in a much quieter hotel than the 'Adelphi', and unless like Isabella and me you had slept in your clothes for eighteen nights you can not imagine the pleasure of a nice warm bathroom and the sight of bread and milk to the children. We all need rest. When we got back to this cold air again Isabella's cough increased. The children have been very good and contented; Tilly was always 'wishing for Bim to draw us'.

Detail
16 × 18 cm. Watercolour. 25 July 1857.
Hugh with William and Margaret
fishing on the shore of Smirisary.

Tilly added a note at the foot of her grandmother's letter: 'Plates, cups and all the crockery smashed. We got our food in mugs and used our fingers. Chairs were of no use; we sat on the Captain's chests lashed to the table, off which Grannie was launched, forgetting for one moment to hold on. I was very sick and poor Loo most miserable; as Annie said, 'She spitted over everything'. Annie slept for eighteen hours out of the twenty four and took her dry porridge with contentment.'

I used to read the Bible with the children asking them questions upon it: 'What was forbidden in the garden of Eden?' Bill: 'They were not to eat green apples.' This was forbidden in the garden at Roshven. 'What did Joseph say to his brothers when he started them in a waggon to go to Egypt?' Lady: 'They were to take heed not to tumble out on the way!'

When my sister Isabella was reading the Bible to her son Colin he asked, 'Was it wrong of Judas to betray Christ when he was prophesied to do it?' She heard him telling his sister Tilly about Adam being made out of the dust of the ground. Tilly said afterwards to her nurse, 'Mummy has been telling me such nonsense, that Adam was made out of dust. He would been blown away!'

I never like to make the children learn hymns (with a few exceptions). The Bible says 'The Kingdom of Heaven is within us'—the hymns tell us of a happy land far away where, as the untidy schoolboy wrote, 'We shall have ham and eggs three times a day'. Mrs Barbauld tells us in a hymn that the soft grass is spread under the young lambs that they may not hurt themselves in falling. This amiable doctrine is not advisable to be taught to children who live on a sheep farm in the Highlands, where lambs are hurt by falling into bog holes or over precipices.

About this time there were coloured glass windows put into Glasgow Cathedral by different families in memory of their relations. We went with a party to see them and afterwards went to lunch at Pollock. Hugh was about six or seven years old and he sat between Dean Stanley and me. The Dean asked him who put up the brazen serpent. Hugh did not suppose he was being asked so easy a Bible question, and fancying the question referred to the memorial window replied, 'I think it was Mrs Crum'. When the Dean then asked him, 'Who was Oliver Cromwell?' he answered, 'A king but not by right'. The Dean seemed fond of talking to children.

One day we were at Wishaw by Lord Belhaven's invitation. Dr Ramsay was there and Hugh asked him to pull out a loose front tooth which was troubling him, and stood the operation well. It was Dr Ramsay's first operation. He afterwards became a celebrated doctor at infancy, though he had not taken to medicine till late in life.

Hugh learned quickly to read, and read as easily when the book was upside down as when it was in the right position. He began his education at the High School in Glasgow. When we were at the skating pond one day some of his school companions came about and offered to help him on with his skates. He seemed to be a great favourite with them. One of his teachers told me that he had never met a boy who learned the Latin grammar so quickly. He afterwards went to Eton, then was some time back in Glasgow. He engaged a student to read with him to prepare for Cambridge, a Mr Hunter, who when he had been a tutor before in a gentleman's house, had a dull life, was not treated as one of the family, and was in rather low spirits. Our servants were kind to him and Babby called him 'the poor orphan lad'. He was very happy here and was sorry to leave us. Hugh's first idea when he was a very small boy was to be a Professor of Omnology, and afterwards took a great fancy to be a soldier and called the nursery his barracks. This fancy lasted. He went to Sandhurst after Cambridge, then joined the Inverness Militia and then got a commission in the Buffs.

"strong Gale with a high sea
ship labouring heavily & taking great
quantities of water on board —
Pumps constantly attended."
"The Palestine" Oct 1861 Log Book

Detail
'Storm in cabin', on board *The Palestine*
October 1861.

IN 1860 MY BROTHER George was ill with consumption and was advised to go to Egypt for the winter. He would not go unless I went with him, so I went and took Bill with me, as he was not strong in the chest. Colin Mackenzie went too. I started from Roshven in October, Hugh, a small boy then, went up the loch to see me off. He was very anxious to go with us, but that could not be.

We embarked at Liverpool in the *Palestine*, a Cunard Mediterranean steamer. A great storm was predicted and it came after dinner. Other ships that started at the same time were driven back injured, but we went on slowly. It was an awful night—all were sick. In the morning the steward made me take some arrowroot and sherry. I learned to walk on the deck when the ship was rolling. I tried at first to keep to the same plank but that did not do. One of the mates told me the right way was to fix one's eyes on the horizon and let one's legs take care of themselves (a parable might be made out of that). I got to do so quite well and afterwards astonished fellow passengers in the Channel. I was never sick again—though I have been several times across the Bay of Biscay. I was even well in that worst of seas the Gulf of Lions.

After three days it grew calmer. The Captain told me that all the passengers that were named on the list had appeared on deck with the exception of a Mrs Harris. It occurred to me that it would be fun to dress up and personate her. I had often successfully taken in even near relations by dressing up and blacking my eyebrows and changing my voice. I had made friends with Mrs Hornby's governess so I proposed the plan and she lent me some of her clothes. We told nobody but the mate who thought it would be great fun to take in the Skipper. I dressed myself and proceeded on deck, meeting Colin Mackenzie on the way, who did not recognise me at all. The Captain met me by the way and I introduced myself as Mrs Harris. He most kindly escorted me on deck and laid me on a sofa; some of the ladies came about me with smelling salts. They also did not recognise me although it was a brilliant moonlit night, but looked as if they thought I was a queer fish. After a while I said I should like to go downstairs, so the Captain conducted me with care. At the bottom he was going to take me through the saloon but I said 'No thank you, Captain' and went off. The governess, who with the first mate was in fits of laughter, said to him, 'What?! Do you not know Mrs Blackburn?' He uttered an exclamation and fled—I did not want to make a fool of him before the other passengers.

On another occasion Bill and I performed the dwarf to the great amusement of our friends; the steward could not think what we wanted to get into the pantry for. On one of the few calm evenings we had a concert with passengers and crew and played various games. It was on the whole very pleasant.

We had many passengers. One was a converted Jew with whom I had some conversation. I remember him saying that the tower of Babel was built that people might escape another flood. I said that that story was not in the Bible and offered him a bet which he declined. It is in Josephus.

When we got to some of the Greek ports we shipped canary seed, maize and rats. I was known to like birds and when they were caught they were put into my deck cabin. One morning before dawn I felt something hopping over me but could not see what and went to sleep again. A little later I felt it again, and saw it was a great rat which got behind my carpet bag on the sofa; so I got up, wrapped my hand up and grabbed it. I was wondering what I should do next when I heard someone walking near. I thought it was the steward so called out. A voice answered, 'Coming, Mrs Blackburn.' I said, 'Don't hurry, it is only a rat.' Presently my fellow passenger with the grave voice came in with a stick and slew it. I arranged it on my basin stand in a life like attitude for the stewardess's benefit, as I had heard she hated rats. The adventure made a sensation on board and the Captain proposed that it should be nailed to the mast, but I don't think this was done.

During a storm in the Bay of Biscay a starling came on board and was caught and put in my cabin. It grew tame immediately and sat on my hand while I dried it with my handkerchief. It went to Egypt but died while moulting the following spring.

I used to get up early and go on deck to look at the scenery. My cabin was on the east side of the ship and got the early light. One day I was changing, thinking land was not in sight, when a message came from the third mate to say that if I did not come up soon I should miss Mount Ida, so I hurried up. It was beautiful.

Detail
12 × 16 cm. Watercolour and body colour. 7 November 1861. The capture of the rat aboard *The Palestine*. 'During the night Mrs Hugh heard a rat in her cabin, it was pitch dark but after some feeling she gripped him by the tail and yelled for help. Mr Purvis came to her rescue in his *robe de nuit*; she had the presence of mind to call out—Go and put on your dressing gown—which he did and slew the intruder.' (Colin Mackenzie's diary, 7 November 1861, p. 90).

There were a good many Mohammedan pilgrims on board, a picturesque group who sat by themselves on deck and cooked their own food. I began drawing some of them and others came about me, all wanting to be done. Only one objected, a strict Mussulman; but I got a view of him from my cabin window. The Mohammedans are supposed to object to being drawn as it is supposed to give one power over them.

We had much rough weather and rough seas but at last got to Malta into a quiet harbour. The 15th Regiment was there and Captain Campbell Colquhoun took me rides to the wild parts of the island; and a party of us went in a 'go-cart' to Gozo—a 'go-cart' is a sort of cart with one horse and a mattress to sit on. Captain Colquhoun, Bill and I were the party. At Gozo I bought a black Maltese lace scarf which I still have. We went one day with Dr Wisely to St Paul's Bay and on another were entertained in Captain Hornby's ship the *Neptune* at a dinner and ball.

We re-embarked at Malta on a P&O and got to Alexandria where we had the heaviest rain I ever saw. We engaged a good big *dahabieh* there for the Nile. Our sailors, clad in cotton clothing, got very wet so we lent them some of our blankets, which we did not like to take back for fear of vermin; so we had to make do with railway rugs till the weather was warmer. Bill and I slept together in the ladies' cabin. It was light and airy. I always awoke about five; I don't think I missed a sunrise all the time I was away. The steward used to bring me a cup of strong coffee about six and I did most of my drawings from recollection then, before getting up. I saw many picturesque groups also by the riverside which I did from nature.

Abou Simbel was what I most admired in Egypt; we anchored there for two days so saw it well. It looked very well at sunrise when the light was fair in the faces of the statues. We rode about six miles further and saw the second cataract, rocky like Arisaig point. I saw

Detail
12.8 × 18.5 cm. Watercolour. December 1861. Jemima shooting wildfowl on a small pond close to the Nile. '. . . wounded a hawk but lost him, took off a small stork's leg—brought home a bird like a plover, only blackhead instead of green . . .'
(Colin Mackenzie's diary, p. 195).

Below
13.5 × 18 cm. Watercolour. December 1861. Women collecting water from the Nile—evening.

10.5 × 15 cm. Watercolour. 19 December 1861. '. . . the village itself is disgusting and dirty. Mrs Hugh and Bill went to market with Mohammed and saw a sheep bought, killed—then blown up by a big hole made in one leg until it was tight as a drum, then skinned and sent off, all on the spot—after dinner they went out for a walk but seem to have seen nothing particular, the whole place an Egyptian Carstairs Junction.' (Colin Mackenzie's diary, p. 196).

a camel's skull with a raven sitting on it. I brought the skull home and have it now, I have often drawn from it.

The Mohammedan fast of Ramadan is very severe, especially on the working classes. They may not drink, eat, or smoke from sunrise until sunset. The upper classes eat during the night and sleep in the day time. Some of our crew tried to keep the fast. It put them all in a bad and quarrelsome temper. One man in a rage tore his garment from top to toe and had to sit down and sew it up again. Some of them went in swimming, dived, and took a drink that way.

We began our return journey and met with the Prince of Wales and his party at Thebes. We met them walking about and made obeisance. The British Consul, Sir James Colquhoun, was one of the party; and as we were beyond the reach of post or telegrams he brought me a telegram to say that the Professor had typhoid fever and a second to say he was better, which was a great relief.

On Sunday 16 March we heard there was to be a service in the great ruined temple, so Bill and I went. Dean Stanley officiated. After the service the Consul introduced us to the Prince of Wales and invited us to have lunch with them. I was asked to sit next to the Prince. After lunch we were all photographed. The Prince sat Bill, to whom he had taken a great fancy, beside himself; but unfortunately the photographer had to push him a little further back and his attitude was not so good as it was when the Prince arranged him.

The day after this we all rode together to the tombs of the kings and to a ground full of mummies, of which one was dug up for the Prince—a small one of the Roman Period. Bill scrambled about with the Prince over fallen idols. We lunched there, and discovered we were thirteen in number; so the Egyptian who attended to the commissariat was put at a table, or rather a big stone, by himself to avoid bad luck. It had no effect, however, as General Bruce who was the oldest of the party, and was in charge of the Prince, took fever and never reached home. I was well acquainted with his family, the Elgins, in Scotland and found him a charming, perfect gentleman.

The Consul arranged that our *dahabieh* should be towed down river by the Prince's kitchen and horse steamer (there were no public steamers on the Nile, only the Pasha's) so we joined the party for three days.

The Prince visited in our boat, unconventionally stepping adroitly over the rails. Our dragoman, had he known in time, would have laid a carpet and put up the rail. He was much astounded and asked, 'Was that really the Prince of England?' I told him it was, and he could hardly believe me when I told him the Queen went about barefaced and dressed like any other lady. On this day the Prince was dressed in light grey, just like any other young gentleman. He sat for a while and rolled up a cigarette and gave it to Bill who deliberately lighted

Detail
15.5 × 23 cm. Watercolour. 16 January 1862. '. . . when we did get up we saw a view—south one mass of green strath with the blue river winding thro' it and the pink Arabian hills . . . east . . ., green, green, green melting away into the horizon haze, with the river and hills, west of it desert for miles and miles of yellow sand and barren hills behind . . .' (Colin Mackenzie's diary, p. 264).

Overleaf
Photograph taken by Francis Bedford in the Great Temple, Karnak on 16 March 1862, showing the Prince of Wales' party with Jemima (far left) and William (far right).

18th March. 1862.

and smoked it. The Prince said, 'Does your Mama allow you to smoke?' He then invited Bill to dinner. General Bruce asked me if he should look after him as he said the Prince, out of mistaken kindness, sometimes gave his young friends too much wine. I said there

was no need, and heard the next day that the dinner had been a great success and that Bill had been very happy, but had eaten little and would not have his wine glass filled again. He played with the Prince's monkey who bit him slightly, but he did not mind. These tailless apes are horrid creatures. Lord Londesborough had one when we met, that invaded our boat, and I did not like it.

One day our heavy boat delayed the kitchen steamer till two in the morning so the Prince could not get his usual dinner but had to feed on what they had on board. He was quite good humoured about it. When we departed from Royalty we fired all our guns and he waved his hat. They had saved us about three weeks' weary waiting on contrary winds, and in light of the telegrams from Glasgow I was anxious to get home. It was not fitting that we should be taken all the way back to Cairo.

After parting on the Nile we plodded on slowly to Alexandria. The only ship I could get was the *Euphrosyne*, a London boat bound for Liverpool. They said that it had no stewardesses. I said I did not care, if it was seaworthy, which they said it was, so we took our passage to Malta. We started in fine weather. I was sitting reading a story book on deck among the Captain's pigs which were running about, when I found myself nearly upset. The sea had become very rough all of a sudden. Very bad weather came on and we were some days tossed about in wind and rain. Every now and then the screw stuck—I did not like it. At dinner the steward was handing me tomatoes and wheeled round and sat down involuntarily, still holding the dish for me to help myself. The Captain also tumbled. The ship rolled very much and I was cast from one sofa to another with books and ink-bottle on top of me. At night it was awful: my cabin door was open to the saloon, which had a lot of water in it which rushed in and out of my cabin, carrying off my brown leather boots and bringing them back with a clump against my berth. The waves clashed hard against the ship and Bill thought we were bumping against rocks. After two days of this a man went aloft to look for Malta and said it was '*Mafeesh*'. At last we got there, I unfit after how many days' tossing. It was delightful to get into a quiet harbour. I went to Mrs Orde's and occupied their spare room at Fort Ricasoli. I spent a day there and when a P&O came on the second day we boarded for Marseilles. We fell in with some Englishmen who could speak no French, and I had to assist them as best I could to buy a penknife. The Marseillais don't speak so distinctly as the Parisians; one can't tell except by guessing if they say '*cinque*' or '*cent*'. We got via Paris to London and went to the Judge's[49] house in Princes Gardens. They were not at home. I got into a cab and drove to various relations' houses; they were all away or I should have dined with one or other of them. We went back to Princes Gardens and were fed on the housekeeper's cold mutton. The next day we started for Doonholm;[50] they also were away and had left the house and servants for us. When I got to Glasgow I found the Professor better and he soon got quite well.

It was very curious afterwards when we went to London that we could not get near the Prince. On one occasion we were watching him at the door of some exhibition and Charlotte Colvile[51] pushed Bill forward, hoping the Prince would see him, which he did not, and a policeman pushed him back.

I met the Prince again at the laying of the foundation stone at the

Previous page, Detail
22.5 × 28.5 cm. Watercolour. 18 March 1862. '. . . This morning Mrs Hugh went over to the West Bank with the indispensible A.A. . . . [and] went with the Royal party to the tombs of the Assaseef [sic] (where AA was much delighted to find that all the candles had been forgot except his own). Then went and looked at the holes which were being howked for the Prince's excavation—yesterday they telegraphed the Basha for leave to dig, he replied they might dig up the whole Memnonium and take it away if they liked—one Mummy was the whole result, and I have heard it shrewdly surmised, that the Mummy was put there on purpose—Old Mustapha Agha, it is said, directed the digging to be made, so as to be of use to himself by and bye and it is thought will proceed to find something more valuable when the Prince is fairly out of the road . . .' (Colin Mackenzie's diary, p. 451–2). Jemima made a copy of this painting and presented it to the Prince.

half built new College. I was deputed to keep the refreshment room where the guests were received. The Prince was very friendly and introduced me to the Princess Alexandra. He talked of Egypt and deer stalking. I offered the Princess refreshments: she did not answer and I thought I had put my foot in it somehow; however one of her ladies explained that she was rather deaf, and repeated the question and she accepted. This lady then turned to Mrs Barclay,[52] the Principal's wife, thinking she was a waitress, and accepted for the Princess. She seemed to enjoy the sweet things. They had been rather late in leaving Edinburgh and had not breakfasted well. The Princess seemed pleased that her long lilac dress had not been splashed by the mud. After the ceremony of laying the foundation stone the Prince asked after Bill and desired to see him. I heard Professor Rankin's voice shouting outside, 'The Prince wishes to see Mr William Blackburn', so he was found and brought in, very shy in his muddy boots. They shook hands. He said of Bill that he 'was much grown but his eyes were the same.' Bill said afterwards he 'had not been afraid of the Prince but of all the cocked-hatted Generals that were with him.'

The next time we met was at a great ball at Hamilton Palace. We were invited along with all Glasgow. Lord Blythswood told the Prince I was there and he said he would like to see me. 'Shall I bring her to you?' The Prince replied, 'Oh no, I will go to her', so he came, and we talked for about five minutes to the great astonishment of all the Westenders and other grandees who wondered who on earth I could be. He told me he was pleased with the *Britannia* training ship where his boys were and that it was a good education for them. We also talked of deerstalking and of the Clydesdale horse show in which he took an interest. One of the notabilities at that ball was the Prince Imperial. He was a small very active looking man who distinguished himself by vaulting on and off the cart-horses' backs while they were still trotting. Strange that he should have met his death by not being able to mount his horse during the Zulu wars. He was a very nice young man and made a great friendship with John Macleod, the mathematical teacher at Woolwich, who had been Dad's assistant at College. Cooper Penrose was one of our party at the ball, and knew and was very civil to him and kept him for the night after we had left, which was very kind of him; for at Woolwich the Prince Imperial had once thrown some cherry stones in his face, for which Penrose had licked him.

In the year the Prince of Wales had a bad attack of typhoid fever, all the nations were praying for his recovery and strangers meeting in the railway asked each other if there was any news. I was travelling in the railway from Glasgow to Edinburgh. There was a young man opposite me who was telling his neighbour nasty stories about the Prince. When he got out I, being indignant, addressed the story teller, 'Sir, I could not help overhearing what you said to your neighbour. It is impossible for you to know the truth of what you were saying; you, for all you know, may have been bearing false witness against your neighbour.' He looked like a whipped dog. A quiet clever looking man was sitting in the corner; he seemed much amused and at the

49. Colin Blackburn, Baron Blackburn (1813–96), Hugh's elder brother.

50. Colin Blackburn's estate in Ayrshire.

51. Charlotte Colvile (1823–?) seventh of the twelve daughters of Andrew Wedderburn Colvile.

52. Wife of Dr Thomas Barclay.

journey's end when we all got out, took off his hat and made a low bow. When the Prince was at his worst I was waited on by a newspaper agent who had heard of my meeting the Prince in Egypt. Of course he was dismissed without an interview.

IN 1863 BILL HAD MEASLES twice and went out too soon to school and had rheumatism and delicacy in his chest. We consulted Dr Jenner[53] about him, who advised a warmer climate for winter; so he went to Mentone with the Miss Colviles and Alice and Frank and Mary Wedderburn, who were to keep house there until their parents returned from India.

53. Sir William Jenner (1815–98), Physician in ordinary to the Queen, 1862. Established the difference between typhus and typhoid fever (1851).

I joined them with Lady and Hughie at Easter. Bill had made great friends with Traherne Moggeridge and told him much about me, so I found a ready made friend when I arrived. We went out sketching together and when I went long walks with his father I brought him home flowers which he drew beautifully. He afterwards wrote a book about the flora of these parts. He also studied and wrote a book about ants and trapdoor spiders. When I met him afterwards in London he showed me the specimens of the trapdoor spider's net with its ingenious trapdoor. After spending some years at Mentone he died of pulmonary consumption. He was a nice young man and wonderfully patient during his illness. He had been strong and active till he caught a cold in England.

We enjoyed our time at Mentone very much, and took long walks over hill and valley, one as long as twenty seven miles with 'Old Mog' as we used to call him, whose great pleasure was to guide strangers about.

Charlotte Colvile gave Bill a dog, a puppy of the mongrel breed, used as watchdogs and to travel with *vetturini* and guard the carriage. It was a quaint beast and went out sketching with me when I went out about dawn in order to do my drawing while there was still some shade to sit in. I remember a carriage passing and a lady looking out who called him *un chien délicieux*. His name was Besom which means, I believe, coarse grey cloth. He was slate coloured with a bushy curved-up tail.

The Professor joined us when the college vacation began in May, and we went home by France *vetturino* fashion, stopping in the Auvergne. The Professor did not wish to be encumbered with a dog so Besom was left behind with a girl who had been our kitchen maid. Bill was so unhappy at leaving him, and was haunted in his dreams by fear that Besom should be seized by the police as they are very strict about mad dogs, that the Professor went, while we were at Giandola, and brought him back. He was a great amusement to us on the journey. The railway guard said he was too large to go in the carriage with us, so he was put in a dog box where his grey nose was to be seen through the air holes. We were allowed to take him out and give him water at the stations, but otherwise he had to be chained and muzzled.

At Giandola the nightingales had arrived and were singing incess-

Detail
18 × 13 cm. Disraeli's election to the
position of Rector at Glasgow
University.

antly both night and day. In the middle of their concert I heard a
blackbird sing and thought how beautiful its song was. At home I
never thought its song equal to that of the thrush.

The election for the Lord Rector of the University was always an
exciting time in the College. The first rector speeches I heard were
delivered in the Old College hall; but that was afterwards found too
small to hold the numerous applicants for seats, so it was held in the
city hall, firstly for Lord Elgin. He came to lunch with us as I was
an old friend of the family.

The Duke of Argyll was afterwards Rector. He was one of the small
men who had a fine voice and was a splendid speaker. When our
friends brought him to the College it was too late for luncheon, so
I invented an entertainment in the shape of afternoon tea, which was
highly appreciated. I first made his acquaintance then, and admired
his beautiful hair, which was like orange coloured glass silk, and fine
features. Noel Paton was with us and he remarked that the Duke had
a Presbyterian delivery.

Among the College Rectors' speeches I have heard, Lord
Palmerston was the worst; he had no notion of what was required
of him. In talking with his secretary, Astley Cooper, beforehand, I
had said that the speech needed to take at least an hour. Palmerston
was not prepared for that, nor was he ready. He hesitated a good
deal and to fill up the gaps said, 'Now gentlemen'; he repeated it
so often that the students began to laugh. He did much better in the
evening at a workmans' political meeting when an address was presented to him, and better still at a breakfast given by John Burns where
his repartees were lively.

The greatest of all our Rectors was Disraeli (Lord Beaconsfield). His speech was delivered in a large glass-house in the Botanic Gardens. The point of his speech was that young men should find out what their vocation was and act accordingly. Drops came down on him from the roof occasionally and he wiped them off with his pocket handkerchief; it was black edged to show he was in mourning for Lady Beaconsfield. I have always worn one of that pattern since, in memory of him. He had afternoon tea with us one day. He seemed ill and tired and had been at the College chapel previously. On another occasion he had lunch with us. On the way down to the dining room with me he talked of the right way to hand a lady downstairs (always on his left arm—so that his right was free for his sword). He partook of some oatcakes which he said was 'food for the Gods', and asked for some butter which did not happen to be on the table. Grace, the table maid, went for it and he turned round to her and said,'I am sorry to give you so much trouble'. He always said kind things to people; when the students were going out and in he would graciously make remarks to them.

I had a great wish that he should pat our pet dog Besom, who was decorated with a blue ribbon bow in his tail for the occasion. I asked him if he liked dogs. He said he did, so Besom was introduced and performed his tricks while Dizzy smiled blandly (I did a sketch of it afterwards, a copy of which the Queen now has). I had no other guest to meet him except John Burns.

After lunch Mr Dalgliesh, with whom Lord Beaconsfield was staying and who was with him, wanted to take a drive through the streets of Glasgow to show him off. John Burns suggested going to see a launch of a small steamer on the Clyde, and rather to Mr Dalgliesh's disgust, this was agreed upon. I believe he would have rather stayed with us and rested before going out to Kier. We went in Dalgliesh's carriage. Dizzy and I sat under a beautiful leopard skin rug given him by a South African chief. Dalgliesh sat opposite, rather cross! The road was long and rough. We talked of Lady Howard and her love of a rough sea.

When we got there Mr Aitken, the ship builder, was astonished and delighted and took us into his sitting room. There was a jolly good fire and Dizzy declared 'it was quite the climate of Palermo'. The tide was not quite up so we had a little time to wait. Mr Aitken brought him a comfortable armchair. He declared it was 'adding scent to the violet'. Hugh was with us and he talked to him about the Waverley novels and the Latin quotations in them. While John Burns was out of the room seeing about the preparations he asked me if that was the Mr Burns who had taken Lord Shaftesbury a cruise in his yacht. I said it was. So when J.B. came back he told him he had heard of it from Lord Shaftesbury who had been much pleased. At last all was ready and we went out arm in arm and stood on planks and saw the ship launched. It was a cold dismal day. Then we hurried back as Lord Beaconsfield had to go to Kier that day to visit Sir W. Stirling Maxwell. When we were leaving, Mr Aitken gathered all his workmen at the gate to cheer as we went off.

While waiting in College I showed him some of my Egyptian sketches. He most liked one of an Arab shepherd boy sitting on the overturned head of a memnon. He asked me to do a copy of it for him which I did, and also gave him some of scenes in the College, which he hung in his sitting room at Hughenden. His secretary Montagu-Corry (afterwards Lord Rowton) told me when I met him some years after at Pau, that in his will, when he ordered his pictures to be sold, some of mine were to be kept; and I heard from a friend who had been to Hughenden that they were still there. Lord Beaconsfield was very tall, about six feet I should think; his eyes were hazel but with a pale edge, the consequence of age, I suppose.

Some years afterwards I asked Mr Aitken to get a man whose father worked at Roshven, Alick Gracie, a place, after Napier's had given up ship building. He recommended him to Murnson, the next best yard, where he was kindly treated and put into the drawing department. They kept him on when the establishment was reduced, and then by it got with the Fairfield works where he gets two thousand pounds a year.

The most remarkable occasion when I disguised myself and altered my face and voice so as to be unrecognisable, was by bright daylight and with only the help of a pair of specs, a thin veil, and a muff. I had gone to the Burns office to enquire about a steamer to Plymouth for my sister. It was the first of April and I asked John Burns if he had been making any April fools. He said, 'No—but would you go into my brother Jamie's room and make one of him? He wants a governess for his girls.' I thought it would be impossible under the circumstances but said I would try. So after putting on the veil and the specs we had a little talk in Jamie's office, and then I said I thought the place would not suit—which seemed a relief to him! However he was very courteous, rubbing his hands in his company manner, and was proceeding to show me out by the public office. I thought that would never do as I had come in that way and all the clerks had seen me. Fortunately it occurred to me to say that I expected to meet my sister in Mr John's office, so I was shown in there where Lady was waiting. J.B. was in fits at my success, having seen my parting with Jamie. After we had gone Jamie said, 'John, what made you send in that old hag in spectacles?—that is not the sort of governess I want.' John said nothing, but when Jamie went out to the country as he did after work hours, he wired after him, 'Do you know whom you have refused? It was Mrs Blackburn!' It was a great joke, for Jamie thought he could take in other people but could not be taken in himself.

Dr Livingstone once came to the College in Glasgow (he had been educated there); he lectured to the students, hoping I suppose to get some recruits among them. He afterwards joined the University Mission—along with my old friend Charles Mackenzie.

When we were at Roshven yachting was a favourite amusement. Our excellent neighbours the Swinburnes[54] used to take us out. The first expedition was in the *White Rose*, a sort of lugger—we went to Loch Scavaig, had a fair wind and a beautiful sail, in the September

54. The owners of Eilean Shona.

Overleaf. *Detail*
24.1 × 31.7 cm. Watercolour with white body colour. 'We break our boom . . . .' The full story of this incident is unfortunately lost; the yacht appears to be hitting the rocks below Alisary at Loch Ailort.

of 1858. Then at the time of the equinox a great wind came. We took a walk round Loch Coruisk and heard a sound like a great waterfall. One of the party who knew the place said there was no waterfall there; it was the wind roaring among the high rocks. We had a very noisy night and had to get down two anchors. Those who could sing entertained us with dismal songs: 'Call the cattle home', 'The white squall' etc. Next morning we had a long weary wait for breakfast. Some oysters, of which there were plenty on the rocks, were gathered, shelled and put on a plate; the wind caught up the plate and scattered them all into the sea. Our friend who knew the country then walked to a farm about eight miles off and got us some eggs. After a few days' detention in the harbour, during which time we walked on shore and got wet (and our English young lady friend got her shoes so wet that the soles came off and had to be mended by our experienced friend), we then set off and warped ourselves out with some difficulty, and set sail. It was very rough. Bill, who was a small boy, remained in the cabin holding on by the handle of a drawer which came out,

14 × 11 cm. Watercolour. 29 July 1870.
Fingal's Cave, Staffa.

and he fell on the floor. One with better sea legs than I went down to see about him and brought up a message that he was very sick but very happy! We stopped the night in a quiet place near Soay and got home with a fair wind and sunny sky the next day.

On another occasion we went a united party in the cutter *Caroline* to Skye—to the Quirang, Storr rocks etc. On entering the harbour to Portree about 10 a.m. on a Saturday evening I remarked to Mrs Swinburne, 'What a fine leg of mutton you have hanging at the stern.' She said, 'Oh, that is not ours, it belongs to the crew; ours is all done.' 'Don't you think we should get some here, for we can't get home for a week?' I asked. 'A very good idea', said she, and turning to Captain Swinburne suggested we should send ashore for some. It took some time for a sheep had to be caught and killed. The rest of our voyage was prosperous. On future occasions I took the provisions and Captain Swinburne the drink. I found that a haggis was a very good thing as it could be warmed up in very rough weather when other cooking could not be done, also a plum pudding and boiled fowl, potatoes; and also cream and milk half boiled so as to keep well. I found at first that the steward used things first which would keep, so I asked leave to order the dinner, an offer which was gladly accepted; and after we fared better.

Another journey was to Staffa, Iona and Mull in a curious centre-board lugger contrived and built by Captain Swinburne. We were out late one evening near Eigg and could not get home as the sea was rough and the winds contrary, so we hauled up the centre-board and deposited ourselves on the sand between the little island and Eigg and had a pleasant night. The *Half Moon* as she was called had been built as a coal ship of wood grown in Eilean Shona. It sailed well before the wind but not otherwise. From Eigg we went once to Rhum with our mast sprung and stopped in the harbour there to get it 'fished'; that is to say, to get it mended with an iron bar. We spent the Sunday on shore in a comfortable shooting box belonging to an absent acquaintance. I had a great desire to go up one of the high hills so I joined the party at 3 a.m.; but before we were ready a thunderstorm began, so all except Bill and me went to bed again. We went out to walk. A high wind rose and we met a man staggering along with a sack on his back. I thought he was drunk but when I reached him the wind was so strong that we staggered too. We often found the harbour in Rhum a harbour of refuge, not that it is good; it is exposed to the north and east and has a sunk rock in it.

Our last cruise was in the *Medina*, a large cutter. We went to call at Inverie. We got there all right but had to leave immediately as the barometric was going down in a remarkable and sudden manner. We struggled trying to round Arisaig point. The sea was very high and when we tried to tack we could not do it, so I was glad to hear the order to run for Isle Ornsay, a sheltered place. We were hospitably received at the proprietor's house by Mr Mackinnon. He had been at Melbourne since its beginning as editor or proprietor of the *Melbourne Argus* newspaper. He was a rich man. He remembered meeting me some fifteen years before on the Killearn railway and what I had said. Crowded as they were, they pressed the ladies of our party to stay and made room in an upper chamber for Lady and me—the gentlemen returning after dinner to the yacht. I rather regretted this arrangement in the middle of the night as the wind made such a dreadful rattling among the slates I could not sleep. It would have been much quieter on the yacht. The next morning was fine and we were shown over the garden, for which I afterwards sent some plants to Mr Mackinnon's sister. We were also shown his horses—very good ones. We had a pleasant sail home.

On one occasion when we got home from yachting everyone had gone to bed, so Hugh who was with me had to get in at a window and open the door for me. I went to bed without waking the Professor who thought Alan had grown very big in the night—he used to sleep with us as a small child.

In 1878 we were just about to start for Roshven from Glasgow, the goods were all ordered and the steamer engaged, when Alan was taken ill. The others started as planned and Grace and I remained

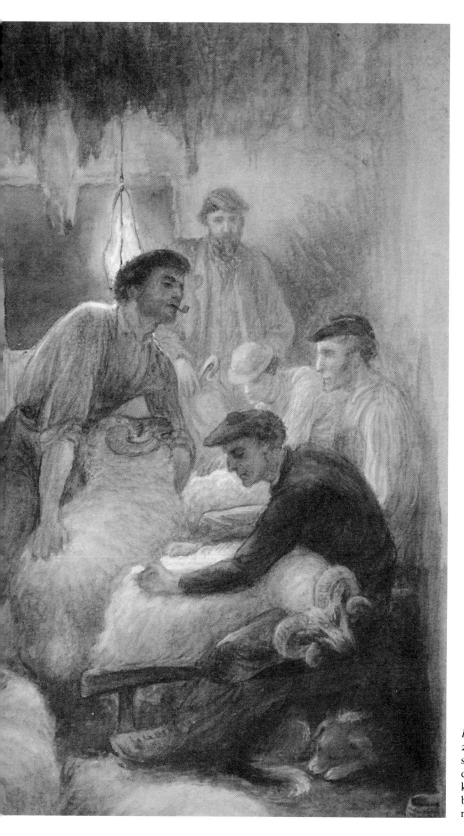

Detail
27.8 × 26.6 cm. Watercolour. Smearing
sheep. Before the introduction of
chemical dips around 1880, sheep were
kept clear of insect pests and parasites
by parting the fleece and rubbing in a
mixture of archangel tar and butter.

Detail
16.3 × 20.3 cm. Ink over pencil. 2 July.
'Incantation.' Anthony Trollope is
second from the left, Jemima sixth;
Iceland 1878.

with him. Mrs Reid our faithful old charwoman came in to clean the house and get in daily food. One morning I got a telegram from John Burns to ask me if I would join him in a yachting expedition to Iceland. I was thinking it over and hesitating when a voice came from the sick bed, 'Mam—you're a greater fool than I took you for if you do not go'. So I accepted the offer.

I first took Alan to Roshven, then went back to Wemyss Bay to join the party. We had one of the Irish boats, the *Mastiff*, chartered as a yacht. The party numbered sixteen. At dinner on the first evening I sat next to Albert Grey (now Lord Grey). He seemed a bit of a dandy and I wondered how we would get on, I need not have worried; we did and very well and were much together during the expedition. Anthony Trollope was one of the party, a rough spoken good sort of fellow; one wondered how he came to write such good novels.

We had much talk and arguments as he was a Liberal; all the rest of us were Tories. One of the arguments with Tony Trollope was whether the world would have had the greater loss by the non-existence of Nelson or Byron. I was on the side of Nelson or course. A.T. told me one day that I was not like any one else he had known—I wish it had occurred to me to ask how so!

On arriving in Iceland (we went via St Kilda), we rode to the geysers taking food and tents and the steward and cook. It was a distance of about 35 miles. Mrs Burns knocked up but the rest of us got on very well. We were supposed to sleep in the church. I could not sleep, so got up and climbed over the pews and sleeping bodies of the party, and got out and met Captain Campbell Colquhoun who was also wakeful. We went to the loch and got a boat and went to an island, where I sketched a pretty little bird while he went to bathe. We saw some long-tailed ducks; one was fluttering as if badly wounded, and he was just going to fire at it when we saw a lot of ducklings swimming about which was the cause of its antics to entice us away from them. We were very hungry when we got back for breakfast and had delicious fresh trout.

We were obliged to return home sooner than planned as there was expectation of war with Russia and John Burns thought his ships might be wanted for transport. It did not come off.

We did not often have visitors at Roshven. The Duke of Argyll came here once in his steam yacht, lunched and dined with us, and went to the islands to see the sea birds. There was a sea fog that evening, not usual here, which detained him for some days. It was the first visit of an Argyll to the MacDonald country. Some of the people began to speculate (for fun) on how soon a band could be collected to take the yacht, and settled it might be done in a couple of hours. We used to have music in the evenings. The workpeople came in and sat in the passage to hear it and usually applauded greatly. On the evening after the Duke's yacht left there was no clapping. Alice Wedderburn[55] who sang to them was rather vexed, and asked them if they had not liked her songs. They said they had, but that 'Bhan', an old fisherman's wife, had advised them not to applaud anything but Prince Charlie tunes in fear that those they did not recognise should be Campbell ones. She was an ardent Jacobite.

We used to visit the Duke and Duchess at Inveraray. On one of our visits Gladstone had been there just before us. Lady Constance, then just a little girl, said to her mother that Gladstone was not fit to be a member of Parliament as he wanted to cut down her favourite tree, a forked one they all enjoyed climbing on. Another visit was just after the Queen had been there; we got her room which the Duke and Duchess saw us to personally. The bed had a slope on it and Dad fell out or nearly did so. I remember once being urgently invited by Lady Victoria to come to Inveraray. The Duke had been taken ill in Glasgow and was convalescing and she thought it would help amuse him. It also gave her some rest and time to look after her poor people. We went out driving daily and watched the numerous birds with an opera glass and had much talk in the evening. The only other person who was staying was the Duke's son who was very affable. He took me to see his Arab horses.

Another visitor to Roshven was William Thomson (Lord Kelvin) in his yacht *Lallah Rookh*. His party included Miss Cram, Mrs Watson, Miss Whittaker, and a Sicilian, the Marquis San Giorgio, who wished to see the Highlands. He was a sportsman and had a wish to shoot grouse, which he had eaten but never seen alive. I tried to get a neighbour's game keeper and dogs but could not, so we took out a very old dog of Bill's, Sweep. I took charge of him and helped him in the rough places as he was very ancient and feeble. Lady had very good sight and could mark down the grouse, and our shepherd carried the bag in case we should be lucky enough to find any game. The dog had very good scent and soon came on a covey. The Marquis hit right and left and was much delighted, and in fact danced a jig. The shepherd was much astonished to see a gentleman who knew

55. Alice Wedderburn (1852–?) eldest daughter of Andrew Wedderburn.

no English and 'could only speak his own Gaelic'. We went on and got more of the covey and a hare or two. It was a very hot day and we were lightly clad and got quite wet when a thunder clump came on. We went home to an early dinner.

In the evening I proposed to him to go out fishing. On the way to the boat he pointed out his clothes to me, and asked my opinion of them and if I thought they fitted him well. I said I thought them very good homespun, and that they didn't fit him very well but were otherwise not remarkable; and wondered why he spoke of it. He then told me they were the Professor's and that his own were all wet! We caught a lot of lythe and saithe, and he thought the fish very naïve to be caught so easily. Another day he shot rabbits on the island. All our conversation had to be in French. Even had my Italian been good enough we could not have got on, as he and Mr Whittaker (the wine merchant from Marsala) always spoke Sicilian to one another. Lord Kelvin had taken the yacht and gone for a cruise with the others of the party and Alan, a very small boy then, went with them. They were absent for some days and then returned and took away our guests.

Some years after, when we were visiting Palermo, I did not like to write to him as I thought him too great a swell; but after we had been there for ten days or so I met an English lady who was in society and knew Italians. I asked her if she had met him, and she said often and that he *lived* in Palermo. I asked her to tell him we were there and he came to our hotel that very evening. He entered smiling and talked of all he had done at Roshven. He seemed to have forgotten nothing from the *Tête Brûlée de Mouton* to the white rabbit, Alfonso, which I had asked him not to shoot. He was very vexed we had been in Palermo so long and had not let him know. He proposed taking us on a drive the next day and we went to various places which we had not seen. We went to 'The Park', a pretty place but not tidy like an English or Scotch one. He stopped the carriage and produced cake and wine, and we sat on blocks of stone and regaled, clinking our glasses. On another day he brought his *chiens d'arrêt* to the hotel to show me ; I drew them for him.

On a subsequent visit when I was there with Pam he came to see us and asked us on to his *maison de campagne*. His father, who had been a very celebrated archaeologist, had died, and he had succeeded to the Dukedom of Terradifalco and a country house, a very pretty place but not at all like a ducal mansion in this country. A queer house with brick floors, but with comfortable chairs, books and beds with handsome covers hung on them.

Twice again when we were at Palermo we went and stayed with him, visits of which I have sketches in my books. He consulted us on what we should like to eat and if we should like *le 'tub'* in the morning. Two women waited on us to put us to bed and he lighted us to our room himself. Tea was brought in the morning. He has a farm and a garden where he makes wine, oil, and preserved fruits, and sells green peas. We were introduced to his household and their children and were much attended to. I had a drive in a painted farm cart. He is well up in Shakespeare, and Ossian's poems, which are much admired by the Italians ; he is also fond of the Waverley novels and was much amused at my giving all his staff names out of the novels ; the old valet and factotum I called Caleb Balderstone. He talked of them as his *queue*. One went about with a gun slung on his shoulders. I asked him if it was for brigands—no, it was only *de luxe*. Our conversation was still only in French. He had some friends to meet us at lunch one day. One Sunday we went to a beautiful villa and garden to tea with the Mazzarini—great swells, with nice children. The Count fortunately spoke English quite well, as also did his old mother. Another day we went out in a hired sailing boat with bare footed sailors. He likes the sea and would have been a sailor if it was not for his old mother, now deceased.

He was planning another visit to Roshven but unluckily was prevented at the last moment, after breaking his leg in Stockholm. He has since sent us mandarin oranges, the first from his garden, and preserved peaches—the best I have ever eaten.

When first leaving the College in Glasgow to settle at Roshven we used to go abroad for a time in the Spring, to France or Italy or Sicily. Of all our tours abroad I think I enjoyed one of the last, that to Greece, the most. We had a very pleasant voyage. We stopped for some days in Corfu in a charming and comfortable hotel where English was spoken. One waiter, who looked like an Englishman, and was always very clean and up early, seemed to address everybody in his own

16 × 18 cm. Watercolour. June 1856.
Birds fishing, Loch Ailort.

language so fluently that I at last asked him to what nation he
belonged. He told me he was Italian. The Greek ships were good.
In one there was an English engineer to whom we talked when we
were stopping near the place of the Delphic Oracle. He told us he
had come for six months to take charge of the steamer, and said he
was from Carlisle. He spoke much of the beauties thereof, which
hardly seemed appropriate in that magnificent scenery. He was long-
ing to get home again.

At Athens we were lucky enough to find Lord Bute at a hotel near
us. We arrived there in Passion week, and on Easter Sunday he called
and together with Lady Bute took us out a walk. He was a capital
cicerone. He took us out on his lovely yacht to Aegina and to Eleusis
and other places. On Easter Tuesday we went to the dances at Megara
where we saw a sort of reel danced by Greeks in Albanian white kilts,
more elegant than Highland ones and more decent, having under them
dark blue tights. On leaving we were invited to sleep in his yacht,
the *Esperanza*, which lay in the harbour close to our steamer.

On the anniversary of our golden wedding Lord Bute gave me a
beautiful bracelet copied from a Greek one in the British Museum.

The last time I saw him in London I lunched with him in his beautiful house in Regent's Park. We went to the zoo by his private entrance
to see a Siberian sledge dog, which he wanted my opinion of before
he bought it for Lady Margaret, and to see some baby monkeys and
lemurs which interested him. I did him a sketch of them, with some
difficulty, as they hid themselves in the straw. I had to do them mostly
from recollection, only getting glimpses of them at intervals. I have

Detail
13 × 18.5 cm. Watercolour. 8 May 1857.
Arrival at Roshven. The paddle steamer
is anchored in the lee of Goat Island.

always liked Lord Bute. He is very original and thinks for himself,
a fact, some Catholics do not appreciate. He is much interested in
Natural History, is a great archaeologist and a lover of beautiful works
of art.

We were acquainted with Mr James Baird who had taken a farm
and found minerals on it, by which he made a great fortune. He was
very sagacious with a strong sense of humour and a great love of the
poems of Burns. He bought Cambusdoon in consequence. He also
bought a large tract of ground from the Glengarry family and settled
there. We used to pay him an annual visit as it was within a day's
journey of Roshven. We went five miles by boat, then about twelve
across the hill, then met his boat on Loch Nevis. We took a ghillie
with us to carry our knapsacks. We could usually make the journey
between breakfast and tea time. Mr Baird had no objection to talking
of his former way of life, and described his first day's hunting com-
ically; how at the first leap he had described an arch in the heavens
and had fallen heavily on the other side, like a sack of meal. He never
hunted again though he kept very fine strong horses. I sat next to
him at dinner. He wore a large diamond stud in his shirt front. We
talked of the comparative merits of tea and whisky as a restorative;
he recommended tea during work and whisky when it was over. Every
time we visited him he said something amusing or wise to remember.

One year we had a visitation of the typhoid fever here. My sister-in-
law and her children came for a visit, and she arrived rather tired
and could not think what had made her so, as she had only walked
a little bit of the way. Some of the people here were ill. Babby told

16.5 × 15 cm. Watercolour. 12 July 1856. Left to right: Isabella Blackburn (Pam), Hugh, Rebecca Blackburn (Menie) and Jemima behind the umbrella on the track between Glenuig and Roshven.

me that Donald looked like a man who had had fever and thought he would be the better of driving here and having some beer. He did so. The doctor, such as he was, said that the people had feverish colds. One of our men was bled and drank five glasses of whisky but recovered in spite of all. My sister in law had her eldest boy to sleep with her but he was so restless we moved him to another room. She did not seem ill but did not get well. After boiling down all our fowls for soup we sent to Glasgow for some beef. We had no fit boat crew, so I took one of our number to Ardnish to try to get a man there to collect our beef from the steamer. They had a long talk in Gaelic

Oct' 8 1857

and after a while I asked if he agreed. My man said, 'He has said nothing yet'. At last he agreed, so when the beef came he had it down at the landing place and rowed to what he thought was a safe distance and shouted!

Miss Macloughlin was with us and was a good rower, and when we expected Miss Blackburn[56] of Doonholm to come to help look after her sister she and Donald, now partly recovered, and I rowed the boat to Kinlochailort to fetch her. She did not come. All the people there were anxious to avoid the infection. The gamekeeper's wife, a friendly person, put out cups of tea and bread and butter for us on the road. We did not go to the inn. It was summer and long light. Donald said that we could wait no longer as the tide would soon turn and we would not be strong enough to row against it. We set off, leaving a message for Miss Blackburn to be taken in, when we would send the boat again. We had hardish work getting home—it took us two hours at least—one able bodied man would have done it in half the time.

When we arrived the Professor was on the pier and told us that Helen was worse. I went to her. She was slightly delirious and thought her sister upset on the road, a rather dangerous one, and I could hardly persuade her to the contrary. When Miss Blackburn did arrive she undertook to be nurse, but finding she could not stay awake I was called back to duty again. When I sat up all night I looked forward

12.5 × 17.5 cm. Watercolour. 8 October 1857. Vaccinating against smallpox in the fields at Roshven.

56. Isabella Blackburn (1817–?) eldest daughter of John Blackburn, known to the family as Aunt Ba. She lived with her brother Colin and never married.

to hearing the birds begin to sing in the morning—the wren was generally the first. Eventually we sent to Glasgow for a doctor. Our neighbours, the kindest of people, would not lend us a trap, they were in such a black funk. So we sent a man and horse so far, to meet him. When he arrived he pronounced it typhoid and gave us directions, saying that it was nursing, not doctoring, that was required.[57]

One day I was told our old handyman was looking ill. I went to see him. He seemed to have lost all the little English he had, and while we were talking he fell prone on the ground. The Professor and I lifted him into his bed, from whence he did not rise for months. Being always rather underfed he benefited by the good care and feeding and recovered; and I am glad to say is still with us.

It was not known at that time that milk conveyed infection. Our dairy was quite a clean place, but the woman who milked the cows had fever in the house. Our kind neighbour Mrs William Robertson received our children at Kinlochmoidart. I used to ride over and see them when I had time and generally fell asleep in the saddle while setting out from there.

57. Despite, or because of the doctor's instructions, Helen died at Roshven. She was married to Robert Fergusson of Kilkerran and after her death their three children were brought up at Doonholm by Colin and Isabella Blackburn.

Detail
17.6 × 22.5 cm. Watercolour. January 1885. Margaret 'skating'.

EPILOGUE

JEMIMA'S MEMOIRS end abruptly in both versions, and she never finished the task of setting them in final order. Her health was failing but nevertheless the house at Roshven continued to be a focus for the younger members of the Blackburn and Wedderburn families. The daughters of Andrew Wedderburn's youngest daughter, Margaret, May and Joanna Wedderburn Canaan, visited Roshven every summer. They were young, intelligent, full of fun, and adored Roshven and their Blackburn relations. May, in an extraordinary powerful and gently nostalgic autobiography, remembered these years:

'I first went to Roshven in 1897. The Roshven boat with four men in red shirts, blue coats and tamoshanters with red bobbles, came up to the head of the loch to meet us. The railway stopped at Fort William then and we drove in a wagonette from there to Inverailort, lunching on Scotch broth at our cousin Hugh's house at Corpach. Tired and stiff with the long drive we were carried in the arms of the huge boatmen across rocks slippery with seaweed, and put gently down in the boat, wrapped in rugs, and rowed the five miles to the bay. There was a tumbled pier of large boulders, a boathouse with a garden, sea pinks on the rocks, and then the house, cool, dark and full of flowers. (The room we all slept in had wall paper with swallows and apple blossom, and we at once 'owned' the swallows that flew beside our beds.) The dormer window had two steps up to it and arrived there, we saw beyond the water the long line of the Scaur of Eigg and peaks of Rhum. There was breakfast in the gunroom for the children and friendly, smiling, Highland maids. There was Lady. It was Heaven.

'It was very remote. There was nothing passable by a wheeled vehicle after the road stopped at Inverailort. If it was too stormy for the boat the ponies came over the hill and, clutching a bag with your night things, you rode.

'On the Moidart side the track went along the shore to Glenuig, a few crofts where they fished a bit for the herring, and the School;

and then on to Samalaman and its Island; but turning left it went steeply across the hills above Loch Moidart and Eilean Shona to Kinlochmoidart.

'We went up every year for Joanna's birthday in May and there was always an expedition to Goat Island to pick primroses for the hospitals in Glasgow. Packed in huge wicker laundry baskets they went up to the top of the loch by boat and on by cart and rail.

'There were cows up at "the Square" where the cowman lived in a thatched hut with an earth floor, while the new cottage great-uncle had built for him remained unoccupied till he should decide that he would not perish with cold if he lived in it: or died. His daughter lived uncomplaining with him; waiting.

'The Square held also the stables with the farm horses and the Highland ponies we rode, and the big barns full of oats and straw and hay. Each cottage had its stack of peat from the hill, and the coal came in the coal ship and was tipped onto the shore at Coal Bay and brought up by cart.

'There was a dairy where we were allowed to help, turning the handle of the big churn and listening for the butter to begin to say "wallop"; and ducks and hens that lived in the grassy wood between the house and the shore where the burn runs down through the garden to the bay. (Rosie, the grey donkey we thought was especially ours, lived in a field up the avenue and was turned out on the hill with the horses at the week ends "to keep them together".) Up and all over the hills were the sheep. The shepherd lived in one of the cottages by the Shepherd's Burn, and Ronald the gamekeeper lived with his gentle wife Katie in the cottage at the far avenue gate and played the pipes. On the night we arrived he came, after we were in bed, and played welcoming tunes under our window; and the night before we went away he came and played "Lochaber No More", and "Wull ye no' come back again?"; and three little girls lay in bed and cried because tomorrow the train (the railway had been built on to Mallaig then) had been asked to stop at Lochailort and it was time to go south.

'Our great uncle, Professor Hugh Blackburn (he had been Professor of Mathematics in Glasgow), had white hair curling down to his shoulders and a white beard and was nearly stone deaf. Our great aunt, who was called simply "Mam", was going blind and he would allow no one else to cut his hair. She was a known painter in her day—a pupil of Landseer and a friend of his and of Ruskin—and especially distinguished for her paintings of animals, one of which hangs in the Art Gallery in Glasgow. She designed a stained glass window for Glasgow Cathedral, and windows with the Nativity and the Shepherds watching their flocks in the little church at Kinlochmoidart. An ornithologist, she illustrated several books of birds: *Bible Beasts and Birds; The Crows of Shakespeare; British Birds*, and *Birds of Moidart*.

'The house was full of her paintings some of which we coveted quite dreadfully, and it was also full of books; when it was too wet even for us to go out we used to lie on the floor of the Painting Room (which was really the Library) and read. You had to know your way

19 × 15.2 cm. Jemima, photographed by
T. R. Annan and Son c. 1885. She is
wearing a hand made and painted
costume designed for a fancy dress ball.

about the books especially when Cousin William, the Professor's eldest son, and his wife were staying there. Cousin William had read for the Bar, but suspected of T.B., was really a dilletante. He could mend everything, but despised you so much for breaking whatever it was, that you never asked him to mend it. He had a sarcastic, not to say bitter, tongue, talked a good deal in quotation, and when he had declaimed one, snapped "Quotation?", and you had to supply chapter and verse. Brought up at Oxford and accustomed to people who said "claptrap", he did *not* frighten us, but it was terrifying for strangers who often did not come again if "Mr William was up".

'But before the railway came to Lochailort the great excitement of our early days was when the steamer came in. She came from the Isles, bound for Clyde; MacBrayne's steamer the *Clansman*, or the *Claymore*, hooted and slid slowly past Round Island dropping anchor under the shelter of Goat Island that lies across the mouth of the bay. All the men would have knocked off work and been waiting for her in the boats. *St Mungo*, the Roshven boat, *Zebedee*, the fishing boat, the big dinghy, and Lady with an excited trio of children in her little *Mab*.

'All the dry stores for the house and the cottages came in the steamer; sacks were lowered down carefully into the boats, rowed to the pier where the two gardeners hauled them out, and the boats turned for another journey. The crew were always much amused at Mab and her crew and a sack of flour or sugar would be lowered into her with much joking, and "Och, an' it's a fine little boat she is". When it was done the great steamer pulled up her anchor with a rattle of chain, hooted goodbye and went upon her way.

'If the weather was too bad, or the great, green Atlantic swell from a storm far out to sea was pulling itself up on the back of Goat Island, she would hoot twice and turn south, and then at the end of the month, there would be a shortage of sugar, or biscuits, or flour.

'The food was stored in the big attic that ran the length of the house; and on Mondays Lady "kept shop" for the cottages, selling everything at cost price, and sometimes we were allowed to help, weighing things on the enormous scales.

'Everything else came from the garden or the farm, or from the sea or the burns. We all learnt to fish, and when we were older and Mam had a house-party and wanted trout, or maybe mackerel for breakfast, Lady would say, "You children go out before your supper and get a few mackerel, but don't go beyond the fishing rocks". Or we would go up, if it were trout that was wanted, and fish one of the burns; or sometimes, with Lady, up to the hill loch with the cliff where the golden eagle built.

'When I was grown up I was fishing by myself one evening and a shoal of porpoises, like me after a mackerel, came in and took my line. Being brought up mostly as a boy has its compensations for of course I had my knife (and not just a pen-knife either), and as he slewed *Mab* round and made off for Skye I cut it, and all was well.

'Chiefly we lived on mutton, greens from the garden, fish and fruit; and of course "real" scones, with marmalade, for tea. There was hardly ever cake.

'Everyone dressed for dinner though it was only mutton, or maybe a chicken or a duck, and a wonderful pair the old people looked; he with his white hair, and she in black velvet, with the family diamonds if there was a party in the house. There were always flowers for everyone, buttonholes for the men and posies for the ladies, and on the 25th of July, the anniversary of the day the Prince landed, there were white Jacobite roses. An Englishman staying jokingly refused to wear his . . . perhaps he feared he might be asked to drink to the King over the water. He was never asked back.

'We always did our yearly play in the laundry for the children on the estate, and Lady took endless trouble for us over the clothes and the "props", providing screens and backcloths and furniture, and a huge tea for everyone after.

'There was also the dance when Hugheena played the accordion and Ronald the pipes, and we danced reels and the Flowers of Edinburgh, and Petronella.

'There was no one like Lady. She taught us to row, attended patiently while we learnt to swim with water wings and finally to dive from the rocks, and then to dive from the boat and climb into her again; and when I had to swim, with a very slow breast stroke, the mile to Goat Island because a cousin had done it, she rowed beside me so that I should not drown. Endlessly she took us picnics; to the islands up the loch where the seals breed; to Goat Island when the running seas were breaking on the rocks on the outward side, and

Detail
18.8 × 27 cm. Watercolour. Stoat eating
the carcase of a heron. One of the
illustrations for the long planned, but
never completed, *Animals from Nature
or Fauna of Moidart*.

From Life

17.3 × 18 cm. Watercolour. On the shore in front of Roshven House, inspecting a catch of skate. Left to right: Hugh, . . .?, Hugh jnr, William, . . .?, . . .?, Alan, . . .?, Jemima.

the spray flying over our heads and the top of the island, fell on the inland shore where the eider duck had her nest. Later, when we were older, she took us across to Ardnish to the Singing Sands, though only when there was a flat calm. Even then she would watch carefully. On one day, halfway through tea, there was a slap of a wave at our feet, and she said urgently, "Quick, children, into the boat". Well, we were quick and got off in time, but I don't think I have ever been more frightened in my life than when I was rowing in that great green swell, come in so quickly from the Atlantic after a storm far away at sea.

'She steered herself that day, a small figure, bright-eyed, calm, determined; saying "You must row steadily, children. We must go up the loch and turn under the lea of Burnt Island." Down in the great green hollows one could see nothing but walls of wicked green water. Obviously, one must not catch a crab or miss a stroke though at times there seemed to be no water one's oar could reach. She was extraordinarily skilful and she knew her sea, but it must have been anxious . . . .

'When it was wet we took tea to the hut by the burn, which we had built of stones and barrel staves and roofed with turves and heather. Or we went to Carnmore Cave where the men were sent every spring to lay clean straw for the tramps who used it for sleeping in, going over to Glenuig or Loch Shiel.

'On Sundays the Professor read prayers in the dining room and we all attended, but when we were older we rode with Lady, side saddle in long habits, over to church at Kinlochmoidart. The birches and the rowans dropped silvered rain drops on us in the early morning sunshine, and the ponies put their feet together and slid down the Plat rock, where the Jacobites buried their silver that they had brought to sell for the Prince.'

Neither Hugh nor Jemima were the type of people to resign themselves to old age. Hugh continued to run the estate, although he had to rely upon Margaret for many of the day-to-day decisions, and inevitably these did not always meet with his approval—a fact that he seems to have regarded with faint amusement rather than annoyance. On the rare occasions that she was away from Roshven his letters to her are warm and humorous.

24th Nov. 1892

Dear Lady,

I got yours of Sunday (10th O.K.) I have been busy (or perhaps I should say occupied) with paying wages and making up accounts and the only things I had to say to you I thought would keep—perhaps improve by keeping. One fact is that so far as we have seen Mary Anne is going to be a great success—she cookes potatoes far better than Christina and most other things quite as well and seems to enjoy her new work. The other thing I have to say is that I was rather taken aback when I asked if the girl (who you told me was coming from Slochd for laundry) had come and they told me you had changed all that and it was one Joanna from Smirisary that was coming. You should have told me. Then presently I was told there was a 'hitch', that you had arranged that Mary Anne was to take charge of the distribution of the milk still—but her successor was still to clean the dairy dishes and do out the dairy : and that Joanna said she would not do it as Miss Blackburn had said nothing about it. I saw I must intervene and so I interviewed Joanna—asked her what wages you said she was to have (you should have told me them) and by great effort heard her say £8. I could not hear any more so she went and fetched Jeenie and then I said—It appears you were to get the same wages as Mary Anne had, you know you would have to do what Mary Anne did. It does not in the least matter what Miss Blackburn said or did not say, you must do as much of the work Mary Anne did as we require (or words

Detail
25.8 × 26.8 cm. Watercolour. 12 July
1865. Two ponies on the hill above
Roshven House. Looking north-west
over Loch Ailort to the Ardnish and
Arisaig peninsulas. In the distance are
the hills of Skye.

14 × 19 cm. Watercolour. 7 September 1875. Left to right : Margaret, Alan, Mary Wedderburn (the youngest daughter of Jemima's brother Andrew) and Jemima taking their leave of Captain Robertson outside Kinlochmoidart House.

to that effect) where upon Joanna agreed (or Jeenie reported) and the incident was closed. But the moral is that I should have been informed before you left (which I wasn't) or that you should have stayed till the 'new woman' was installed. The incident rather worried me—but I fancy it will all go smoothly now.

Your Dad H.B.

A letter which arrived one Christmas met with an immediate reply.

25 Dec 1902

Dear Lady,

. . . I read your letter to Mam, received today, with reference to a statement in which I think your Dentists bill is rather an extra which I might pay—Practically I am writing to the National Bank to place £20.00 to your credit which I hope will make it easier for you to make any visits you wish without overdrawing on the Bank. You may consider this a windfall from Santa Claus.

Your affectionate Father,
Hugh Blackburn

Not all his correspondence was on such a mundane level. He and William Thomson, Lord Kelvin, kept up a brisk and erudite exchange of letters discussing anything from the rigidity of ether, or the metric system, to grand opera.

Jemima planned a companion volume to *Birds of Moidart*. The much discussed idea of producing a book on animals was resurrected yet again, with the proposed title *The Fauna of Moidart*. She had, of course, sufficient paintings with which to illustrate the book, and got as far as writing (and having typed) a manuscript to accompany them, before once again the project was shelved. She also wrote a play with strong Jacobite overtones, possibly planned for May and Joanna to perform during one of their summer visits.

The old couple were becoming increasingly frail and the world into which they had been born had changed radically. They were no longer in touch with the rapid advances in the arts and science. Scott, Raeburn and Beethoven were all alive in the year of their birth; but by 1909 Picasso had completed his 'Blue Period' and had painted '*Les Demoiselles d'Avignon*', Schoenberg's Chamber Symphony had caused riots at its first performance through its abandonment of traditional tonality, and James Joyce had published his first collection of lyrics.

Sadly Jemima's health deteriorated rapidly. Late photographs show her only in an invalid chair, and it seems that she slipped into senile dementia. She died on 9 August 1909. Hugh, who was two months and one day younger, survived her by exactly two months.